The Event Manage

A Complete Step by Step Guide to Successful Event Planning & Organizing

Diane Bartlett

Disclaimer

The content of this book has been checked and compiled with great care. For the completeness, correctness and topicality of the contents however no guarantee or guarantee can be taken over. The content of this book represents the personal experience and opinion of the author and is for entertainment purposes only. The content should not be confused with medical help.

There will be no legal responsibility or liability for damages resulting from counterproductive exercise or errors by the reader. No guarantee can be given for success. The author therefore assumes no responsibility for the non-achievement of the goals described in the book

Contents

INTRODUCTION

"To achieve great things, two things are needed: a plan and not quite enough time." -Leonard Bernstein

Event Management is the process of planning, organizing, promoting, executing, and assessing a gathering of people or an event. It is a unique method of advertising a product, service, or concept to the public. If a product or service launch or marketing event is conducted quickly and successfully, it may be a highly effective promotional tool for launching or marketing a product or service. To justify a professional approach and create successful and efficient outcomes in events management, certain basic values must be applied to every aspect, process, and decision. In the context of personal or business events such as festivals, conferences, ceremonies, weddings, formal parties, concerts, or conventions, event management is the application of project management principles to the conception and growth of small and/or large-scale events. It entails researching the brand, determining its target audience, developing the event idea, and arranging the technical parts of the event before the event is officially launched and promoted.

Events of various sizes presently take place in the events sector, ranging from the Olympics to business breakfast meetings. Industry, celebrities, charity organizations and interest groups all arrange events to sell their products, create commercial contacts and generate funds. They also hold events to recognize and commemorate achievements. In the event management industry, the process of organizing and managing the event is referred to as "event management." This process can include budgeting, scheduling events, site selection, obtaining necessary permits, coordinating transportation and parking, booking speakers or entertainers, arranging decor for events, coordinating with third-party vendors, and developing emergency plans. Because each event is unique in its own right, managing and executing each event varies depending on the kind of event being managed and executed. The event manager is the person in charge of the overall planning and execution of the event and the responsibility for the creative, technical, and logistical parts of the event. Event planning services cover everything from overall event design to branding, marketing strategy to audio-visual production, script writing to logistics, budgeting, negotiation, and client support. An event planner is a relatively new discipline that encompasses all of the preparatory processes needed in the professional administration of a convention or other event such as a ceremony, meeting, negotiation, party, or other gathering.

Event planning is not for the faint of heart or those who are rigid in their thinking. To be successful, it is necessary to have excellent organizational and communication skills, understanding of the sort of event being planned, a strong network of trusted connections, and, most crucially, the ability to adapt to last-minute adjustments. When it comes to the many responsibilities of an event planner, negotiating prizes and budgets and securing qualified speakers are only the beginning of what they do. Professional event management services oversee all essential utilities, set tables, seats, laptops, and even take care of the details such as picking appropriate décor for the event. For unskilled event planners, event management may be full of surprises; as a result, effective event management necessitates the development of thorough emergency plans if anything goes wrong.

Chapter 1: Pre-Requisites of Event Management

Planning and staging an event, whether it is a meeting, business event, fundraising gala, conference, convention, incentive or other special event, has been likened to filmmaking. Still, it is more like putting on a live stage show, according to some experts. In the absence of a safety net, it's a high-wire act. It is not possible to reschedule your event after it has started. There will be no dress rehearsals since it will be shot in a single taking. To re-shoot a scene, you must call "cut." Your visitors and suppliers will interact and respond in ways that you will not be able to foresee, as you would be able to do with a film screenplay. Although it is impossible to predict the future with certainty, it is possible to plan and be prepared for the unexpected. Nothing can go wrong, and everything will go wrong, according to Murphy's Law. An event that went wrong was when a crew from the event planning, staging, and lighting setup departments showed up days before the event to set up an elaborate poolside event complete with a dancing water light show and music display at a privately owned venue that had been poorly planned.

As a result, they were horrified to discover that the swimming pool had been filled months before they arrived, but that no one had informed them of this. Furthermore, the event planning company and their suppliers had not returned since contracting to conduct a pre-event (pre-con) meeting, nor had they specified swimming pool requirements in their vendor contract or event function sheets. Extensive decor and a lavish fireworks display were brought in at the last minute, at great expense to the event planning company, to create a new fantasy look that would appease their client, who did not need the added stress of a last-minute change just days before a long-anticipated special occasion. Even though you are not producing an Oscar-winning film, it is always vital to remember that you are doing something that may become a lifelong memory for someone. Whatever the size of the event, whether it is for 50 people or more than 2,000, it must be planned as meticulously and meticulously as a film production, and the budget must be as well. Meeting and incentive budgets may range from tens of thousands to hundreds of thousands of dollars. It is extremely usual to see budgets in the millions for corporate events, product launches, conferences, conventions, incentives, and other special events.

Event planning is considered successful if there are no surprises on the day of the event and at the time of final reconciliation. The event programs exceed its stated goals and targets. Before planning any event, you must first identify why you are hosting or participating in it. This is referred to as "definition of the event goals," There may be both main and secondary objectives in a single event, depending on the circumstances. In the following section, we will go over the objectives of the event in greater detail. Having a clear understanding of why this event is being held will assist you (and your client) in laying out the company or client objectives—both tangible (day-of) and intangible (long-term) returns—so that you can then select the appropriate event style to deliver on those objectives. Using a business convention as an example, a company can participate as an exhibitor, as an attendee, or as an event sponsor; be represented by a company speaker; attend seminars; or host a gala farewell, a hospitality suite, or an evening event for select conference attendees, to name a few possibilities. A company's time, money, and energy investment in each of these event scenarios will provide a different return. It is critical to determine which kind of event will deliver the most value and create the greatest outcomes in reaching the company's goals.

1.1 Defining Your Event Goals

For an event to be successful and provide a return on the time, money, and energy that the business hosting the event has invested, it must be carefully planned to fulfill guests' expectations and the expectations of the company hosting the event. When planning an event, you want to build excitement, encourage maximum guest attendance, and encourage complete involvement in embracing both the major goal and the secondary message of the event. Whether tangible or intangible, event objectives can be met before the event (if, for example, a qualifying sales objective is required in the case of an incentive programs), during the event, and after the event, and can serve as a bridge, platform, and positioning to meet the next level of objectives for subsequent events. An event aim must be valuable to the business hosting the event and to people participating in the event. It must cross over from professional to personal rewards, as well as the other way round. In one instance, a corporation sought to organize an event—or a

9

series of events—that would encourage its employees to be more productive, raise morale, minimize workplace accidents, and lower the amount of money they spent on health insurance per employee.

1.2 How much money do you have to spend?

The first thing you should do is figure out how much money you have available to put away for the celebration. Even the littlest event requires a significant financial investment. It is possible that you may not be able to finance an event at this time, or that you will need to take a different approach to get the outcomes you need. Remember, it's better to be patient than to attempt to arrange a substandard event on a tight financial budget. To return to the conference example, it is possible that your event dollars would be better spent having company employees attend the conference as participants—where they are free to network during the day and not confined to an exhibit—and hosting a unique, private, upscale dinner exclusively for the key people with whom you want to spend quality one-on-one time during the evening hours. If your firm chooses to sponsor what would otherwise be a low-budget "gala" meal, it may increase its awareness, but it may not represent the image of the company you are attempting to convey.

Wouldn't it be preferable if you could spend your available event dollars to entertain 50 or more guests in the manner you know is required to impress your target audience, rather than trying to stretch those same dollars to cover decor, entertainment, food and beverage for 1,000 conference attendees, the majority of whom your company will not do business with, and in the end producing an event that is not in keeping with your company standards? As soon as you have established your event goals and chosen the most appropriate event style to achieve them, you will be able to strategically plan an event that will be specifically tailored to fulfil those requirements. For example, in The Business of Event Planning, you may discover clear strategic design concepts that I have developed, as well as strategic planning case studies. The second choice to be made is to determine the scope of the gathering. This will be determined by two factors: the amount of money available and the goals. An example is a supplier who pulled off a dinner event on the stage of a well-known theatre (which was closed to the public for the evening) with the stars of the show in attendance and putting on a private performance for them that was the talk of the conference the next day and made their company stand out from the competition.

It was an event that made its guests feel like celebrities, and those who were not invited hoped to be included on the elite guest list for next year's event. As well as making business connections with conference attendees, they hoped to do so with company employees who, because they were there as attendees rather than staffing an exhibit booth, would have time to step out of the conference with prospective new clients and enjoy multiple coffee breaks, lunches, and other activities without being constrained by time constraints. This firm produced more industry awareness and won more future business via a two-tiered event strategy than they would have if they had spent the cash, they had available at this specific conference and at a different time of the year. It was simple for them to determine which sort of event would best suit their event aims after taking stock of their company's objectives, both short- and long-term. It is important to always know how much money you have to spend ahead of time to choose the suitable event style and organize the event to stay within your budget. Before doing anything else, it is good to make a preliminary estimate of expected costs and inclusions. This is because, very frequently, budget approvals from higher-ups are necessary before an event can be approved. By creating a preliminary budget based on your event vision wish list of inclusions, you will be able to determine what will be feasible and what will not be feasible for your event. In the case of a firm arranging an incentive program and wishing to spend seven nights in a certain location, they would be able to immediately evaluate whether or not the flight consumed the bulk of their budget. If this is the case, they may have to consider if a three-night stay, which would allow them to remain within their budget while also assisting them in achieving their objectives, is worth it.

The decision to require a seven-night stay would necessitate the imposition of additional fees and restrictions. Perhaps they would have to find a more convenient venue, or they could have to come up with a means to raise additional money, such as by asking sponsorship from industry or supplier sponsors for certain event features. Other methods of increasing their event budget or looking for other creative, cost-effective solutions may be required. This may include partnering with another company and designing an event that creatively combined what each company could bring to the table to produce an event that would be a standout could be among the options. Millions and millions of dollars' worth of diamonds were brought in for a very premium book launch glorifying glamour, and visitors were encouraged to enjoy wearing them and being photographed while they were there.

One lady wore diamonds worth more than 20 million dollars for her once-in-a-lifetime picture shoot, captured on film. Two guests slipped out a side door that had not been secured to enjoy a private dinner in the hotel restaurant, which caused concern for the event organizers. The diamonds were brought in by Brinks trucks and 20 armed guards, and the event area was transformed into an apparent diamond-dazzling fortress (but remember Murphy's Law—two guests slipped out a side door that had not been secured to enjoy a private dinner in the hotel restaurant, which caused concern for the event organizers). However, although the effect of the diamonds, worth millions of dollars, was significant, the expense of having the diamonds on-site was little.

Upon midnight, all of the diamonds were returned. The only hard expenditures associated with this successful event element—where the goal was to represent a luxury experience—were insurance, Brinks trucks, armed security, and the services of a professional photographer. And the luxury jeweler business that provided the diamonds ended up selling some of the diamonds to guests who had attended the event the next day, resulting in a profit for the store. For the business, it was an opportunity to showcase their diamonds to a highly focused audience and a marketing move that resulted in a significant increase in sales and the attraction of new customers to their jeweler store. Because of their innovative method to attracting attention to their shop, they invested just moderate hard expenses. The smallest amount of money was spent on generating the greatest possible one-of-a-kind event impact. The book publisher, the author, and the jeweler shop all benefited from the successful event collaboration.

1.3 Event Vision

It is critical to start with your client's original event vision to build an event that will meet their goals and be all they dreamed it would be. This is the stage at which you will discern what is most essential in their lives. Event visualization is the beginning point for every event design project once the event's goals have been established. Even if you wind up at a completely different location than you had initially planned, sketching out your event vision on a grid can assist you in beginning to lay out your event budget needs. You might begin to calculate backwards from the supplied budget to check whether there is a match or if more flexibility in the budget or event needs to be discovered before moving further.

For example, one corporation had a budget of $4,500 to spend on a luncheon event for 250 people outside. Tents, tables, chairs, linen, dishes, silverware, and food were all listed as expenses, as was entertainment and a modest take-home present, according to the information they were given about the budget. Their idea was to host a picnic in the spirit of New Orleans. Their budget allowed them to spend just $18 per person on everything listed above when it came down to it. The cost of renting a tent for 250 people, including installation and deconstruction, and permits and insurance, would easily surpass the whole budget of the event. If staying with a New Orleans theme was determined to be the most important factor in helping the company achieve its event objectives (for example, if they were launching an incentive programs to New Orleans), a creative event option would be to take over a local jazz club on an exclusive basis and work with the facility to create decor, entertainment (taped or live), a menu, and an open-bar package inclusive of all taxes and service charges that would allow them to come in under budget and keep their guests entertained. If staying with.

Chapter 2: Elements of a Successful Event Management

When organizing any event, the first step is to take a step back and look at the broad picture. Before setting your event date and even looking at locations, you must first visualize what you want to achieve. It is critical to take a step back and look at the needs for your event that have concrete expenses and must be included in your space request as part of the entire picture. The most effective approach is to organize everything on a grid that is centre on the week of your event. More information on how to use this grid will be presented in a subsequent chapter that deals with the needs for location. It is your event overview grid that will offer you significant information into your budgeting and event schedule as well as logistics and orchestration, all of which will influence your final decisions. It is a handy event planning tool that will change as your event progresses, and it serves as the foundation upon which all of your event's aspects will be constructed. To ensure that you can make corrections as you go, we recommend that you work in pencil, or create your grid on a computer spreadsheet.

Produce additional copies of your original event pieces so that you may experiment with them, arranging them in several ways to discover the ideal fit energy-wise, and that your event culminates with a grand finale and finishes on a high note. Your event grid worksheet will guide you through deciding which event elements to include and how much money to allocate. When designing your event, bear in mind that each aspect has an impact on the others. If one aspect of your event is neglected, a domino effect might arise, jeopardizing the event's overall success. Preparing an event overview grid from the beginning of your planning process and tweaking and updating it as you go through your plans can help you avoid crunch moments and any surprises down the road. By planning ahead of time, you will be better prepared to deal with any last-minute adjustments that may arise. Timeliness, logistics, and orchestration of all of the event parts leading up to your actual event, on the day of your event, and in the days after your event must all be considered while planning your event.

These components may include the following: Guests are transported to their destinations. Accommodations for visitors Items are sent off to their destinations. Advance move-in and setup of the venue, which includes rental fees, labor expenses, equipment rental, union charges, lunches for crew, and other costs, in addition to the costs for event elements, personnel, security, permits, insurance, and other costs, are also included. Rental expenses for rehearsal space, labor expenditures, equipment rental, union fees, and food for the crew, among other things. Rent, labor, equipment rental, union fees, lunches for crew, and other expenditures associated with the event on the day of the event, in addition to the costs of event inclusions, personnel, and other expenses. Teardown and removal of the venue include rental fees, labor costs, equipment rental, union charges, meals for the crew, and other expenses, in addition to the costs of event features, staffing, security, permits, insurance, and other expenses, are included. As you visualize your event show flow, begin to pencil in the schedule of event items under the relevant days on your calendar. At this phase, you are not concerned with real scheduling and logistics, but rather with an overview of how you see your event, as well as the days leading up to and after the event, unfolding.

2.1 The Essentials of a Successful Event

"Must-haves" for an event are unassailable items at the time of initial planning and cannot be changed. These expenses are calculated by taking into account the following factors: hard costs, such as airfare and hotel accommodations, space requirements (move in, setup, teardown and move out, as well as storage for suppliers, rehearsal space, on-site office space, and other requirements that are separate from actual main meeting/event function space), meeting/event function space requirements, meal requirements, activity requirements (if any), and all applicable taxes, service charges, permits, insurance, communication costs, staffing, and other expenses (while these cost items can be negotiated and pricing concessions obtained, they need to be included regardless of the final event design and event inclusions) What would be of significance to those in attendance? What would make the occasion unforgettable for visitors is the following: What would best capture the enchantment of the message presented to the audience?

15

Some of the must-haves for an event are not based on monetary value, but rather on emotional currency and how they appeal to your senses. Some are simple to incorporate and cost little money, while others need more thinking, preparation, and financial resources. As you begin to imagine your event, it is critical to establish the must-have elements present. Remember to consider each option in terms of both economic and emotional currency when addressing a need rather than a desire for an event, and think about each decision's consequences. The must-haves for your event will become the focal point of your event design, and the rest of the event features will organically flow from there. While you are building your list of event necessities, you should also compile a list of event upgrades that, if funds are available, might be considered to take your event to the next level.

2.2 Things to Consider When Choosing your Event Venue

People who rush to choose a place before they have visualized their event day from start to finish, identified the must-haves for their client and their event, determined their financial situation, and visualized their event day from beginning to end, risk overlooking a venue that would have been the perfect fit for their event, one that meets all of their needs and is within their price range. Consider comparing hosting a tented New Orleans brunch versus hosting a New Orleans jazz brunch in a private venue where there are no extra tenting or rental fees to consider while working with a $18 per person budget. The initial event concept and the location where the event is finally held might be opposed and even contradict one another. Plan your event around a location solely for the sake of securing a date as soon as possible. You may find yourself sacrificing what is most essential to the event and missing out on something unique. Consequently, you will wind up arranging an event to suit the space available rather than developing one that would achieve the goals your customer is looking for.

We live in an era in which events are held in settings that are only limited by the creativity of the event designer and the organization's financial constraints. On land, in water, underwater (in restaurants and spas in the Maldives, as an example), in the middle of nowhere (on board aero planes), on top of the planet, and in space are all possible venues for events today. Traditional venues include, for example, the following: Mansions owned by individuals (rented or owned) Hotels

Convention centers are places where people get together to exchange ideas. Museums Galleries of fine art Country clubs are places where people go to relax and socialize. Private yachts are available for charter.

However, you have a plethora of possibilities at your disposal. Event venues include theme parks, aquariums, involve a variety, roller skating rinks, theatre stages, private fly-fishing clubs, country clubs, tents in the middle of the desert, private pools covered over for dining and dancing, restaurants that have been taken over exclusively, a soundstage, a converted barn, a plantation home, on a catamaran, a cottage retreat, a country fair, in a retail store, on a mountaintop, in teepees and Transporting guests to event places has included private barges, antique automobiles, and snowmobiles, as well as hay wagons packed with bales of hay, double-decker buses and pedicabs, as well as ferry, horseback, jeep, motor coach, and limousine. Whether you are searching for a typical or innovative venue to host your event, you will need to consider seven crucial factors while putting out your vision for the event itself. More information on the location criteria will be provided later in this book. The size of your guest list will play a role in determining the venue of your event. In what part of the country do most of your visitors reside, and what transportation and lodging expenditures will need to be included in your budget?

How may a national or religious holiday or other special event (such as a sports event, an election, or another unique event)? Even the seasons have a role in the choosing of venues. When the same location is used in various seasons, it might result in a distinct set of logistical and financial issues for events. Depending on the sort of site you pick, every season might provide its own set of difficulties. In the summer, air conditioning, backup generators, and ceiling fans would all be necessary considerations.

In contrast, a heating system or freestanding heaters, flooring, and lighting would all be necessary considerations for a tented event held in the early spring or late fall, when the weather is significantly cooler during the day and night, the grass can be damp and chilly on guests' feet, and the sun sets much earlier. For more information, visit www.tentedweddings.com. The same holds for construction sites. At one occasion, a visitor fell due to the heat in a quaint building that did not have air conditioning, and the event was cancelled. Custom fans were distributed to visitors at another event held in the same area to counteract the heat, and the fans served as a lasting remembrance of the occasion.

2.3 Event Time

The time of day is a key consideration. Will you be the only organisation conducting an event at the location, or will there be a number other activities booked there as well? Will you feel as if you are part of an assembly line if many events are being hosted simultaneously? When an event that is supposed to take place before yours begins late, what occurs is that your event is delayed as well. What happens if their visitors decide to stay a little longer? Approximately how long do you anticipate it will take for your suppliers to set up and for visitors to be granted entrance to the room/venue? If you are the ones who have the earlier time slot, how will you guarantee that your guests leave on time so that the following event can be set up and running? Is it likely that you'll feel hurried and harried, and would it be better for you to host your event at a place where you'll be the only event in the facility, or the only event in the room you've chosen, if you're the only event in the facility or the only event in the room you've chosen?

If you intend to have your event outside without a backup plan in case of inclement weather, you may put your event at danger. In the event of poor weather during your spring, summer, or autumn activities, a tent or a private room at the same location may be rented for you in advance. The same may be said for outdoor winter activities that take place outside. Companies that want to host a ski event must secure a site to move the event if dangerous weather conditions develop. Outdoor events need particular setup and expense considerations. For example, in the case of a tent, depending on your needs, moving in and putting up may take anywhere from two to three days to a week, and it may be further delayed if it rains. It is also necessary to account for the time it will take for the earth to dry.

It may also take several days to dismantle and transfer everything out. Site rental fees for setup and takedown days may be required depending on the location of your event, since the facility would be unable to rent the space to anyone else during those days. If you want to pull down on a Sunday, you should double-check labor expenses since there may be extra fees. Other cost considerations could include having the grounds maintained, or renting separate cooking tents for the caterers if the venue does not have a kitchen available or one that will meet your needs, as well as providing security for your guests. Tents can and have been blown away, and having someone on hand to deal with the situation as soon as it occurs may help you avoid major problems in the future. Another consideration is ensuring that rented goods such as chairs, tables, décor, audiovisual equipment, and other things are properly secured overnight and throughout the move-in, setup, takedown, and move-out days when many people will be coming and departing. For events held in several locations, you must consider the travel time between each venue, whether or not your visitors will be able to easily commute between the two places, and how you want to arrange the arrivals at each location. All gambling establishments are not created equal when it comes to their terms and conditions. Consider that what could be provided at no extra cost at a hotel—tables, chairs, linens, or specialty gasses such as martini glasses for a martini bar—may not be included in the room rental fee in a conference centre, museum, or other similar setting. It is possible that certain objects may need to be brought in specifically for your event, and that a rental fee will be required.

2.4 Event Style & Feelings

Your event's style refers to the overall ambiance or impression you are attempting to create. The combination of several styles might result in something unique. Style is unique to the individual. There are no "should" when it comes to fashion, and fashion is never about money. A romantic event, for example, might cost hundreds of thousands of dollars, if not hundreds of thousands of dollars, depending on the event type or theme you choose. The amount of money you have to spend may restrict your alternatives, but it will never limit your event's design's overall concept or spirit. Your event's style will affect the selection of invites, location, guest clothing, flowers, décor, music, entertainment, cuisine, and drinks, among other things.... The ultimate effect will be a layered ambience that will flow together to create your event's overall aesthetic. Every occurrence generates a certain amount of energy.

The location, décor, music, food and drink, activities, and mix of guests all contribute to the energy in the room and the atmosphere that these elements establish. When you plan your event, you can bring positive or negative energy to your gathering. A space can be physically drained of its energy due to poor design planning in terms of scheduling, logistical arrangement, and related event aspects. This is the sensation you get when everything becomes flat, when there is dead air, stilted dialogue, or uncomfortable silences, and when the room becomes devoid of vitality. When there are unnoticed congestion, lengthy waits, hungry or exhausted customers, and limited seats, negative energy may permeate a space and become overwhelming. It is also possible to deplete the energy in a space by selecting a room or a setting that is either too large or too tiny for the number of guests expected. The Business of Event Planning contains in-depth information on how to stage a room to achieve the greatest effect and energy possible. The event style you choose will be conducive to conveying the emotions associated with your event, so choose wisely. A romantic style, for example, may elicit thoughts of tenderness, softness, and closeness, all wrapped up in feelings of love. With a lighter theme that depicts a lively nature, a lighthearted warmth that is kind and affectionate, as well as a dash of celebration, will emanate from the gathering.

Consider the overall look and feel of the event, as well as the emotions you want to elicit. Identify one that will capture the essence of your event's aims and the feelings that will distinguish your event from the others. Create a thorough wish list on a spreadsheet in Excel or equivalent accounting software that covers everything conceivable, regardless of cost, and enter it into the system. By putting up your budget on a computer, you will be able to evaluate where you stand fast and make modifications to expenses when new prices become available. Adding and eliminating various event aspects will allow you to see quickly how your budget will be impacted as you make changes to it. Draw attention to the headings that are necessary to include in your programs. The other elements are entirely optional and may be included into your preliminary budget once it has been determined. Consider the following scenario: if food and beverage expenses are a must-have, but menus and place cards would be a nice event enhancement, if funds are available; or, if menus and place cards are determined to be important to your company because of its presentation style, you must be aware that these costs must be factored into your preliminary budget in addition to food and beverage expenses. As a result, if your preliminary cost estimates, which include only the non-negotiable items, are higher than your proposed budget, you will need to seriously consider whether you should proceed with your planned event or whether you should look for areas where you might be able to make budgetary adjustments. For example, is it possible to choose a simple meal while still including the menus and place cards, or do you have to stick with a gourmet menu to convey the tone you desire for your event? If your early cost estimates are much lower than your planned budget numbers, you may then begin to consider include your optional items in your final cost estimates.

Chapter 3: Initial Planning to Event Management

A firm or an individual has decided to host a gathering. After preparing an event vision and preliminary cost estimate, they have determined that they have adequate cash and have put aside a certain amount of money for the event to occur. They have defined the event's goal and determined that it will be worthwhile in terms of financial investment. They are now prepared to undertake the preliminary stages of preparation for the event. They will determine whether they require outside professional assistance and will bring in an event planning company, hire an independent event planner to work to their internal team, or have their internal team directly work with event suppliers to handle their event design, budget, logistics, timing, and event execution; orchestrate the event; and help them to visualize the entire event from beginning to end during this phase. When it comes to arranging huge events, far too many individuals think in terms of dollars and cents rather than common sense.

Whether they are corporate, nonprofit, social, or wedding-related, clients must understand when and where to seek professional event planning assistance, such as a public relations expert, a creative director, or a producer, who will oversee the entire event production process from concept to completion. Event planners mustn't promote themselves to their customers as part of the service sector, since that is not their duty; rather, they should be viewed as order takers rather than event planners. As a result, they must present themselves and their company as a valuable sales and marketing tool that can assist corporate clients, nonprofit organizations, and individuals in designing, producing, and delivering an event that is custom created—not cookie-cutter—and strategically designed to meet and exceed their identified company, professional, and personal goals. Even though they are often considered a luxury, event planners and other event-related experts should never be extra expenditures. They may help you save money in the long run, particularly if you bring them in at the right time of the year. For example, a professional public relations firm can assist you with your guest list and ensure that the appropriate individuals are invited to your event; they can also assist you with creating press releases and press kits to get national and international media attention for your event. As a creative director or professional event designer, your job is to offer you a strategic conceptional overview of the event design. This includes planning components such as organisation, logistics and negotiation factors, and those little things that add up to a magical experience. When it comes to event planning nowadays, the sky is practically the limit—and beyond—and experts can broaden the horizons of their clients.

A new golf club has been launched successfully, with an astronaut playing golf in space, to commemorate a magazine's 50th anniversary cover (an oversized mock-up was laid out in the desert and was designed to be seen from space); dinners (or breakfasts, lunches, or cocktails) have been lifted to new heights by being served from a rented dining platform hanging 50 metres aboveground—held up by a crane—which can accommodate 22 guests; and a magazine's 50th anniversary cover has An event producer or event operations staff member ensures that everything that has been imagined becomes a reality. They are also responsible for ensuring that all fire and safety regulations are followed, that all necessary permits have been obtained, and that all necessary insurance has been obtained. When specialists aren't involved, costly mistakes may be made that can be avoided. Suppose you imagine a fire marshal approaching your front door and threatening your event with closure because you don't have the right licenses. In that case, you have too many people for the space available, or you haven't adhered to all safety requirements, you're not alone. How much does it set you back? Or, what is the cost if you host a fantastic event and rely on favorable press coverage to propel you forward, but nothing is done to ensure that it happens? If you are not on top of what is new, fresh, and exciting and the media reports that guests rushed for the exits before dessert was served, how much money do you stand to lose? Companies must be aware of when and when to call in outside experts to assist them.

Try to match talents, areas of interest, and time availability with areas of responsibility when putting together or working with an event committee or team—or both in the case of a firm working in sponsorship partnership with a nonprofit organization—to make the most of the opportunity. Suppose a committee member's job function is sales, and they are expected to continue producing results while assisting with event planning. They may not have time during the workday to go onsite inspections, review guest lists, or be on call when the month closes off and they are under pressure to complete sales transactions. When it comes to Time Management for Event Planners, the needs for event planning time are given out, as are time-making and time-saving suggestions and practices. You want to make sure that the salesman does not feel like a deer caught in the headlights of an approaching automobile. Remember to designate one person from your firm to be in charge of all contact with the event planning company or vendors (if the company or organisation is handling their event in-house). Suppliers are not given competing sets of instructions from several sources, and permission for expenditures is granted to them only by those who have the authority to approve them due to this arrangement.

Initial preparation should involve determining what you will need to accomplish for each aspect, or important phase, of the party and how you will go about doing it. Following up on the list presented in the introduction, the following are the questions that you should ask yourself as you begin to prepare any social event or gathering. Answering these questions, which will be followed by every major phase of the event (which will form the Party Plan), will assist you in moving forward on your journey to creating a great party. In the next chapters of this part, this material is considerably extended and developed upon much more.

What level of work are you willing to put forth? For extremely big or complicated events, you may want to consider recruiting one or more co-hosts to assist you with the planning.

- What kind of event are we talking about? Is there a specific, or unique, theme?
- How many people will be in attendance?
- When should your event take place - what day, what time? Is there anything that clashes with that day and time in particular?
- Is it better to host the function at home or somewhere else?
- What is the time frame? Is it two hours, four hours, or more?
- What do you expect to be able to spend within your budget?
- Identifying whether or not you need assistance, and then employing that assistance – a caterer, a bartender, valets, entertainment, and so on?

- Do you need assistance? In what capacity do you work?
- What resources are available to provide the required assistance?
- What is the estimated cost of the service(s)?
- What are the questions you should be asking potential employees?
- Who should be invited?
- What information do you need to provide with your guests? How many people are you expecting?
- For example, when and how will you announce the event — by electronic mail, Evite, Facebook, or even physical invites?

When should the invitations be sent out? Suppose you believe that the event will be formal or special enough to warrant printed invitations. In that case, you will need to begin the planning process earlier to have the invitations printed and mailed in time and allow for a sufficient amount of time for the guests to respond.

- Make sure to add in the prices of printing, envelopes, and postage into your budget. These expenses are often neglected, but are frequently not trivial.
- What materials and accessories will you need for your next function?
- What kinds of accessories should you have on hand at all times? And how about you?
- What sorts and quantities of beverages will you need - How much wine, beer, and spirits will you require?
- What kind of food, and how much of it?
- What other supplies, outside food and drink, do you have?
- What is the best way to organize your efforts for setup?
- Do you have a need or want to decorate?
- Should I put up the beverages and food for this event?
- Will you be the one in charge of the cleaning?
- What kind of music should you choose to play?
- Will you be in charge of cleaning up after yourself after the event?
- Examining the event's overall success - What lessons may be drawn for the future?

Chapter 4: Types of Events

When deciding on the sort of event to host, consider your target audience's preferences. Even though busy professionals may not be able to take time out of their schedules to attend a symposium that will interfere with their designated family time, if the event is specifically designed to include their family members, such as a private screening in a theatre or an exclusive booking of an entertainment centre, they may be able to attend. The symposium may be conducted in the morning when their children are in school or playing with their friends. They may meet for a catered luncheon after which they will have the remainder of the day to enjoy the facility with their family members; alternatively, in the case of a private showing in a theatre or premium seating for an in-demand live show, the symposium could be held earlier in the day, with a private reception before and after the meal serving as an anchor for the entertainment component of the event.

To construct an event that would generate pre-show media attention and hence draw customers to their door, a public event organizer may opt to collaborate with a firm or companies who will assist them in achieving their aim. For example, a bridal show that hoped to attract couples, their families, and their wedding parties to their event included a million-dollar wedding cake exhibit as part of their promotion. As in the case of the glamour book launch, a jeweler firm donated diamonds that were utilized to embellish a magnificent wedding cake, as was the case with the glamour book launch. Every party involved benefited from the publicity, including the television show, the jeweler company, and the wedding cake designer.

Once again, the costs of producing a million-dollar wedding cake were minimal (security, insurance, and labor on the wedding cake), but the returns were enormous for everyone involved. Corporate events, private events, and charity events are the three sorts of events that may be organized. Corporations and consumers emphasize corporate events, while private events are more recreational, and charity events are held for charitable purposes. The most successful business events are those that have specific and attainable objectives linked with them. This is understandable considering the high expense and extensive preparation that goes into each one of them. In this part, we'll go through the top four most valuable sorts of corporate events that you may attend. Detailed information on each kind is provided, including a brief description of what it is, which business objectives it is best suited for, what sorts of venues you'll need, how to organize your event layout, and real-world examples from major companies that you can truly learn from. Let's get started straight now!

4.1 Conferences

In the business world, a conference is a significant event (with attendance numbers often in the hundreds or thousands) centered on a particular subject or industry and is typically conducted over several days. Speakers, exhibits, competitions, networking opportunities, and more recreational get-togethers before and after the conference are all part of the event activities for this sort of gathering. Conferences often draw big audiences of at least 100 individuals, most of whom are genuinely enthusiastic about the subject matter. The purpose of the conference is to discuss a certain topic and create awareness about a specific problem in the community. Following that, a period of discourse around a connected topical problem is initiated to ignite a movement for change.

It is customary for one or more speakers who are specialists in their field to address an audience comprised of professionals or individuals interested in a shared topic to speak before them. In contrast to a conference, a congress draws participants from all around the globe. Speakers from outside the nation are invited to share the platform at this sort of event. Conferences or congresses may last anything from half a day to a day and a half to many days... The size of your event determines everything.

In comparison to other events, conferences are often far more complicated affairs with several speakers and sessions spread over various locations inside one or more venues. Conferences are one of the most fruitful types of business networking events because they encourage conversations and provide people with a platform to share their expertise. Typically, conferences begin with a keynote session before interviews, roundtables, and panel discussions, among other activities.

4.2 Seminars

On the surface, seminars and conferences seem to be quite similar. The most significant distinction is that seminars are exclusively devoted to education and training purposes. Given their academic character, it seems natural that they are generally done in series and include fewer groups than their more huge and diversified event type rivals, which makes sense. Informative events, such as seminars, help companies engage with their customers by providing them with practical knowledge and tools and skills that they can use to attain their objectives. Follow in the footsteps of The Academy of Business Leadership and make an effort to reach underserved population groups (in this case teenagers and young adults). Concentrate on alleviating a single main problem and then supply a plethora of really beneficial answers that they can take away from the encounter. The seminar, which is well-known among businesses, is intended to bring workers together and create a special link between them.

It is concerned with human beings and their characteristics. It is also a wonderful opportunity to express gratitude to workers for the hard work during the year. It functions as a management tool in and of itself! Organizing a corporate seminar may be a good way to boost communication among a team while also looking back on a expired time. It is also an excellent venue for discussing the future and setting new goals. Organizers often choose to conduct the seminar somewhere else from the workplace, however the location will vary depending on the event. Integration seminars, which are designed to ease the transition of new workers into their jobs, are often held on-site.

Motivation seminars, on the other hand, are intended to energies personnel. As a result, it is advisable to perform things outside of the normal working day by offering creative and unique activities! Adding team-building exercises to a workplace seminar may help to keep things interesting and keep things interesting. A seminar is an event that is planned with a particular target audience in mind to deliver highly relevant information. Such an event may be organized at a community centre, at the corporate headquarters, or even online using a platform such as Zoom or Vimeo, among other locations. Because most seminars either include a single speaker or a limited number of speakers, researching possible speakers and engaging potential sponsors should be high on your seminar preparation agenda.

4.3 Corporate off-sites & executive meetings

Corporate off-sites and corporate meetings are face-to-face gatherings that often include high-level workers and/or significant business partners to facilitate communication. Companies hold this type of event for a variety of reasons. Still, the event planner's responsibility is to ensure that they are successful by establishing clear agendas, creating creative environments, and implementing tools or policies that increase productivity. Corporate off-sites and executive meetings aid in facilitating communication and the provision of a greater degree of cooperation that cannot be achieved just via email and Slack. Even though we hear the phrase "corporate event" all the time, do we understand what it means? Simply said, a corporate event is an activity that is organized by a company and is meant for its workers, customers, stakeholders, a charitable organisation, or the general public to participate in. When it comes to events, the target audience is typically determined by what the event is meant to accomplish – such as launching a new product or service, celebrating staff members' accomplishments, or showing expert knowledge in a given sector. Various sorts of corporate events will be conducted on a quarterly or yearly basis. In contrast, others will be one-time activities – such as to coincide with a big announcement or to deliver an award – that will take place just once.

4.4 Company parties

Company parties bring workers together to celebrate shared accomplishments, recognize milestones, raise morale, and have a good time throughout the holiday season. Even though the primary emphasis of this sort of event is often on fun and relaxation, event planners may nevertheless establish and accomplish certain objectives for their attendees. As a result of the inherent morale-boosting impact that company parties have on workers, they are a vital component of a successful corporate event eco-system. It is possible to create entertaining events for your workers even if your company does not have the resources to have a lavish celebration like Amazon's. Make an effort to incorporate items or locations that your crew appreciates as a group or that have particular significance to your company.

4.5 Weddings

Most likely, you are well aware of the enormous responsibility that comes with being in charge of the event planning for a wedding reception, wedding rehearsal, or anything else associated with being a part of a wedding celebration or rehearsal. It is not only the bride and groom who are relying on you to make sure that every aspect of their wedding reception runs smoothly, but the entire event relies on your event planning abilities! Even though it is unlikely that many people will notice if you make a specific faux pax during the reception or wedding event because it is so minor, you are likely aware that you have made a mistake. Listed below are some important details to be aware of when planning a wedding reception or rehearsal dinner and how to coordinate cleanup afterward. When it comes to wedding reception or rehearsal dinner planning, the person in charge of the event may feel overwhelmed by the enormous amount of responsibility placed on their shoulders. The event planner needs to remember that the wedding and everything associated are all about the bride and groom.

However, even though a lot of what is going on will appear to have something to do with the event planner himself or herself, this is likely only the case because there is additional pressure on the individual to ensure that everything goes off without a hitch. Several aspects of wedding event planning should not be taken lightly, including the rehearsal dinner. It would be a good idea for the wedding event planner to persuade all of the wedding attendants to attend the rehearsal dinner for the bride and groom, even though it is not required. Aside from that, another very important consideration when planning the wedding rehearsal dinner is the location, the food that will be served, and the length of time that the dinner should last. Many of these details will be chosen by the bride and groom themselves. Still, the wedding event planner will undoubtedly be required to assist them in making some of the more important decisions, such as where the wedding will be held and ensuring that all of the necessary reservations are in place!

The most enjoyable aspect of wedding event planning may involve witnessing the ceremony and reception to ensure that everything goes smoothly and without any major hiccups! This includes the wedding reception; making sure that the bride and groom have agreed on the food that will be served, the type of cake they will have, and the reception location are all very important aspects of making sure that everyone is satisfied! All of this boils down to understanding that the wedding event is all about the bride and groom. Recognizing this is the key to ensuring that your wedding event planning efforts are not in vain. Even though wedding entertainment is one of the most important aspects of planning a successful wedding, it is often overlooked or added on as a last-minute addition to the festivities. The bride and groom appear to believe regularly that they do not need to put much thought into any wedding event planning because they already know exactly what they want. After all, many seem to believe that tracking down a professional musician or other performer cannot be that difficult. Not to add that, when compared to the costs of the other aspects of a wedding, wedding entertainment activities are often not prohibitively costly.

People tend to feel that anything that is not pricey is typically straightforward to deal with. To put off your wedding event planning, on the other hand, is not a smart option. If you don't offer enough notice to the wedding event provider, you'll probably be dissatisfied since they may already be booked for another wedding at the time of your request. It doesn't matter if entertainment isn't a critical component in the proper execution of your wedding; a wedding without the music of your choosing will not be as pleasant. In general, the shorter notice you give an entertainment provider before an event, the more money they will charge you for their services. You should also allow yourself enough time to browse around.

Consequently, what are some of the many types of entertainment that you may have at your wedding and what are some of the alternatives you have? Hiring a live band of professional musicians is one of the costliest options you may discover for your event. It's easy to wind up with someone who is completely improper for the work at hand if you aren't cautious about who you select - someone like the renowned foul-mouthed wedding singer from the movie The Hangover.

If you make the appropriate pick, you will be able to discover a fantastic professional band that will perform songs from the top of the charts and exciting dance numbers. It may be a wonderful tool for infusing a little romanticism into the festivities. Hiring a DJ to get the party started may be an important part of successful wedding event planning at times. A DJ for a wedding is not nearly as costly as hiring a live band, but it is still more expensive than hiring a live band. On the other hand, putting a DJ up on stage with complicated-looking equipment might be inconsistent with the atmosphere you are trying to create. A DJ, on the other hand, can provide the kind of entertainment that customers want. When you listen to a live band, you are often restricted to the kind of music that the band can produce. When you hire a DJ, you may have a completely different music for every single song. If there is a particular song that one or more of the guests on your guest list particularly enjoys dancing to, a DJ is the kind of entertainment you should hire. Not to add that DJs like hosting little, lighthearted events such as limbo competitions.

4.6 Birthday

Planning a birthday party tailored to the tastes of both the guest of honor and his or her guests is the key to organizing a successful celebration. I earn a good portion of my livelihood by providing live caricature entertainment at parties and other events. One advantage is that I attend many parties, which allows me to see how people plan events to have a good time. A large number of the events I attend are birthday celebrations. And the age of the guest of honor might vary from one to one hundred years old. Here are some real-life examples of birthday parties I visited in my capacity as a caricature artist, for your enjoyment. Make use of these examples to help you come up with ideas for your event. The first event took place on the family's beautiful house, which overlooked a lake. The majority of the event took place outside, with catered cuisine. It had the atmosphere of a laid-back picnic.

This was a family-oriented gathering, with five (!) generations of family members in attendance. Guests were welcome to stroll around the wide covered terrace and the house. People who were more physically active might participate in outdoor activities such as volleyball. People largely just relaxed and ate, enjoying one other's company while I amused them with live caricature sketches while they were at the party. The next birthday celebration was a sit-down meal at a beautiful restaurant. The majority of the visitors were contemporary friends of the guest of honor, with a few members of the guest of honor's family in attendance. The party was gregarious and high-spirited, and they seemed to be having a great time. They sat back and enjoyed the low-key music. It created a lovely environment and provided an opportunity for them to chat. Other instances include: When asked how he wanted to commemorate his 80th birthday, my father said he wanted to spend time with his closest family members. As a result, we devised a method for spending time with his family, which is dispersed around the nation.

As a result, we will go on a short family cruise next year. We were drawn to the notion of taking a cruise since it would allow us to all congregate in one area and allow distant siblings who see one other much too seldom to spend quality time together. A cruise provides opportunities for family members of varying ages to pursue their hobbies while joining together as a family around meal times. Another example is a guy who booked a room at a restaurant and invited many of his friends to a surprise 40th birthday celebration for his wife, which took place in the restaurant. In addition, he arranged for a few male strippers to be on-site over the celebrations. It was a big hit with her. They are both outspoken individuals, and it worked for them. To be honest, this isn't for every person.

The opposite is true: if you know your guest of honor and your guests, and if you work with their tastes, your event will certainly be a success. Organizing a birthday party for your children may be difficult and stressful, particularly if you don't have a plan in place beforehand. Some of you may be wondering to yourself: where should I begin with the decorations or with the food? While worried about preparing the party, you may miss some important details concerning the event. Fortunately, following these steps may make it a whole lot simpler — and more enjoyable. This section will walk you through the process of organizing the ideal birthday celebration for your child. The selection of a theme for a child's birthday party is the first stage in the planning process. While a theme is not required for every party, it is recommended that you think of one to make the event more memorable and to connect with your child's interests and hobbies. As a starting point, think about what your kid enjoys doing or watching as a youngster. These may be used as excellent party themes. When picking a theme, consider other factors such as favorite locations, toys, or figures they like. There will be themes that are simpler to locate party accessories for than others, but it is a terrific chance to be creative and engage the whole family in the brainstorming process!

Chapter 5: What Are the Five Stages of Event Planning?

What is the first stage in the event planning process? Making a strategy is essential! It's right, you read that accurately. If you don't have a well-thought-out strategy for event planning, you run the danger of disorganization, confusion, and failing to achieve the event's objectives. A formula for running a successful event planning firm or one-time event is essential to achieving success. To avoid getting into your next event planning job blindly, use this basic guide to the five phases of event planning to assist you through the process instead.

5.1 Research and Goal Setting

According to the sort of event you are organizing, you may need to do some preliminary research before working on the details. Some event planning businesses may neglect this critical phase, which can spell doom for the event's overall success if done incorrectly. During your investigation, you should speak with the individual or team in charge of hosting the occasion. Find out precisely what their objectives are - whether they are to raise money, educate employees, network with other experts, or share fresh ideas. To improve efficiency throughout the research phase, you should have a list of questions prepared. You'll need to know the estimated budget for the event, as well as the date and approximate number of individuals that are anticipated to attend. After you have finished your research, you may write out the aims and objectives of the event you are planning. To evaluate the performance of your event later on, your goals and objectives should be clear and specific. In addition, this list may serve as a guideline when you begin the primary event planning stages.

5.2 Design the Event

This step of the event planning process involves the creation of a master plan for your event. You'll begin by locating a appropriate location for the event's theme, the number of visitors expected, and the purpose of the event. Throughout the planning phase, you may collaborate with the venue's personnel to improve communication and ensure that everything runs well. Once you've chosen a place for your event, you can begin assembling a group of individuals who will assist you with the

34

remaining design work for the event. In this way, you may take on a leadership position without being overburdened with the intricacies of event preparation. Every member of your team will contribute to the overall strategy. For example, the person in charge of the entertainment will provide you with a list of performers and a timetable of events. The individual or group in charge of food and beverage will present a complete menu and an estimate of the related expenses and a schedule for food service. To assure the success of your event, your event design and master plan must be as precise as possible.

5.3 Brand the Event

A successful event with well-defined goals and objectives should be simple to market and advertise. You are aware of the desires of the event's host and the expectations of the visitors. Make use of your research and your design to establish a brand for the event. But hold on a minute! You'll also need to figure out how to demonstrate how your event is different from others and why it's worthwhile to attend. It is possible to employ promotional materials to increase awareness of your business and get people talking about your event. Do you have a name for your event? Is there a slogan or catchphrase for the company? These particulars may help to increase the success of your event's branding. Consider a name, slogan, and logo for the event as you begin to build a brand around it. The event should make it very obvious to participants what they may anticipate if they choose to participate. As you begin to market the event, your branding will be of great assistance to you. Depending on the event host's preferences, you may utilise an email list, social media postings, or a special invitation list to send out invitations.

5.4 Coordination and Day-Of Planning

Your preparations are coming together well, and you are ready to move on to stage 4 – coordination and the day of planning! Coordination refers to the process of completing plans with each of your team members, as well as with the event staff or volunteer participants. Everyone engaged with the event should be aware of what is expected of them and how critical their contribution is to the event's overall success. You'll be responsible for coordinating the various components of the day's event and distributing the schedule to each team member and your representative at the location. Each event component should be included on the schedule, along with a clear start and completion time. You may also provide the names of the individuals or groups of individuals responsible for each component of the event. Include any other pertinent information on your day-of schedule, such as the person's name to call if there are any technical difficulties. This is a difficult stage to be in! However, it is precisely because of this that event planners are so effective - they pay meticulous attention to every detail.

5.5 Evaluate the Event

Your event preparation checklists have brought you to the last phase - the assessment. Congratulations! There is no universally agreed-upon method of evaluating event planners or event planning businesses. You should utilise the assessment stage if you are new to planning or if you want to gather favorable comments to help you establish your professional reputation as a planner. For conferences and formal job training sessions, you may gather feedback from participants by sending out an online survey or handing out a printed survey to them after the event. Organizers should include questions concerning the event's structure as well as particular goals from your list. However, the feedback received from guests is just a portion of the review. If your team's goals and objectives were not fulfilled during the event, you may revisit them afterward and debate whether or not they were met. If they were, that's fantastic! If you believe you might have performed better in a certain area, talk about it. The best way to enhance your event planning abilities is to be open to learning and developing new ones.

5.6 Successful Event Planning

You now have the precise step-by-step recipe for organizing a successful event. These tips might assist you in remaining organized and on track so that you can get the most out of your event. Maintaining a certain amount of adaptability throughout the event planning process is essential. Things don't always go as planned, and that's OK! If you work as an event planner, you will learn to think on your feet and adapt to changing circumstances.

Chapter 6: How to Plan the Event in the Best Possible Way

The success of any event is greatly contingent on the quality of the event planning. Currently, it has also been transformed into a business, in which individuals assume the obligations of the hosts, provide them with the event that they want to attend, and charge them a fee for their assistance. Event planning is not a difficult task that anybody can perform if they are organized, creative, and dedicated and have adequate time to prepare every detail of their event. On the other hand, some individuals are only happy with their work, and they do not delegate their plans to anybody else and instead complete them themselves. For this reason, if you are arranging an event for the first time, you should do extensive study on event planning to prevent making any mistakes and ensure that the event runs successfully. You should be able to complete your preparations at least two months before the event's scheduled conclusion. This will be a better event to arrange, the more time you have on your hands.

Several preparations must be made, such as selecting a day and location, preparing a guest list, developing a budget, and hiring services like as catering, cuisine, music, interior design, flowers, and lighting, among other things. When planning an indoor or outdoor event, you must first discuss the chosen date with the venue's proprietor to determine if the venue is available on that day or not at least one month in advance. If any adjustments are required, you must notify the proprietor of those changes as soon as possible.

Consider utilizing event-planning software on your computer that will make your work a lot simpler, such as a budget analyzer, guideline sheets, meeting space calculators, registration forms, and checklists, among other things, to make your life easier. Apart from that, several event-planning businesses provide free advice or ideas, which may prove to be valuable for those who seek them. Another part of event planning that must be carefully considered and calculated is the budget. If you do not know how to prepare financial statements, budget analyzer software may help you. All you have to do is total up all of your expenses and double-check to be sure you didn't leave anything out. Maintain a reserve of funds that may be used to cover unforeseen costs.

Aside from these considerations, you must make an informed decision about the future services you will use. It is not essential to seek the costliest services, since they may have defects of their own. Hire people you learned about from a reliable source so that there will be no uncertainty regarding their abilities.

6.1 Best Way to Plan Your Events

People used to arrange their events back in the day when event planning was not a professional sector. However, the event planning business has taken away all of the stress from people's lives by offering them the opportunity to have their events professionally organized and more memorable. Many individuals who want their gatherings to be flawless choose to employ a professional event planner to handle the details. It is a broad industry that encompasses a variety of topics like as wedding planning, corporate meetings, seminars and other events, cruises, field excursions, award ceremonies, and even children's birthday parties, among others. However, some persons are dissatisfied with the work of others and refuse to pass up their arrangement to anybody else, preferring to complete it on their own.

So, if you are one of them and are organizing an event, you should do extensive study on event planning to ensure that you do not make any mistakes and that your event is a success. If you keep these crucial considerations in mind, you will have an easier time planning your event. Time management is the most crucial aspect of event planning; when organizing an event, choose the final date and ensure that you have at least two months to complete the necessary preparations before the event takes place. If you have more time, you will be able to prepare the event more effectively since there are several details to consider, such as the location, cuisine, music, guest list, budget, interior design services, etc.

Whether your event is inside or outside, discuss the date of the event with the owner of the venue at least one month before the event to ensure that the venue is available on that day and that if any adjustments are required, you will be able to make them. In many cases, event planning firms may assist you by offering free advice or ideas; this can be valuable for you as you make your plans. Budgeting is also one of the most critical aspects of planning any event; you must make all of your plans within your budget constraints. Create a budget and make all of your preparations with this in mind. List all of the items you'll need for the event and find out what they're going to cost in the market; you'll find out the pricing of your essential items even if you use the internet to do your research. Make sure to have some extra cash on hand in case you encounter any unexpected charges. Make a checklist for your event; this will help you stay organized. Keep reviewing it often to ensure that all of the work is being completed as required.

6.2 Tips To Highly Successful Venue Event Planning

When planning an event, you must communicate effectively with the venue's contact or event organizer to ensure that everything goes as smoothly as possible. If problems develop during the planning process for your event, you want to iron out as many creases as possible as quickly as possible. Often, this isn't as tough as it seems to be at first glance. In most cases, venue coordinators are more than eager to work with you if your needs are within their scope of expertise. Here are some suggestions on making things go more smoothly and ensuring that your relationship with your venue organizer is a positive one. Make your objectives attainable. The last thing you want to do is disappoint your visitors or yourself by failing to establish realistic objectives for yourself and your business.

Don't overpromise, but be sure you follow through on your commitments. Make a list of everything you want to do and do all you can to ensure it occurs, no matter how difficult it may seem. Small surprises that make you appear like a rockstar rather than a letdown are guaranteed when you are honest about your aims and don't overpromise and deliver. Research. Your research is the most crucial step in your event planning process, and it is the most critical factor in ensuring that your event is a huge success! Examine your options and consult with your vendor coordinator to verify that your ideas are appropriate for the space you have available. Your research will supply you with the knowledge you need to propose the most effective ideas for your event, and it will also guarantee that you get a greater response rate. Make it enjoyable. People despise stuffy and dull gatherings, so make yours as entertaining as possible.

Find creative methods to include suitable activities into your event that will keep your attendees engaged and entertained. If appropriate, you may add hilarious tales, skits, entertaining raffles, or draws in your scheduled event. Consult with your venue organizer about these suggestions to ensure that enough accommodations are provided. Win, Lose, or Draw is a trademark game that I've created for several different occasions. In a box, hat, or other container, the speaker writes down the name of one item on a piece of paper (one for each table at the event) and sets it there for the audience to choose from. Each table will represent a team, and each table will be responsible for selecting a member of their team to draw from a hat. Immediately after selecting, the nominee will have 30 seconds to create a whiteboard depiction of his paper. The other table members will have 30 seconds to guess what he has drawn on his paper. The table with the most accurate predictions wins. This game has proven to be entertaining for visitors, and it is an excellent icebreaker. Create and adhere to a financial plan. This is something I cannot express enough. A healthy budget is an important component of sound planning. When you were doing your investigation, you should have taken into consideration the expense of your requirements. This is what will assist you in developing the appropriate budget. Find bargains and discounts to help you save money and remain inside your spending limits. Now and again, something unexpected may arise that you were not prepared to deal with.

Researching the greatest pricing and making savings to assist you in making up for any mishaps that may occur without going over your budget. Solicit Assistance. Gather a group of friends and family members to assist you with some errands and set-up duties. People will be more than happy to assist you with decorating and collecting up items, as you will discover. Make sure you are in constant communication with your venue organizer so that she is aware of who will be on hand to assist you if the need arises. It will be easier for the venue organizer to communicate with you if anything happens while your assistance is on site. Having assistance can allow you to feel more productive while avoiding the stress associated with your profession as a whole. Add a Personal Touch to Your Order.

If you have a trademark style that you want to include into your events, go ahead and use it, but make sure that any feature you incorporate is subtle and appropriate for the occasion. Suppose your hallmark is to include a unique element into the floral arrangements. Make certain that the element complements the décor and theme of the celebration. Market. Your event's outreach is critical to ensuring that it is as successful as possible. Make use of your marketing abilities to reach the intended audience. Make contact with local radio stations to see if it's feasible to secure a brief mention on the air for your product. In your newspaper, place an advertising for your product or service. Send out invites that are both gorgeous and functional. Many venues provide marketing assistance; check with your venue organizer to see if they do this. The greater the number of channels you use, the higher your turnout. You should send out invites early enough to have a solid response if you are arranging an event that is more of an internal gathering and needs an RSVP. Maintain your composure.

The calmer you stay during this procedure, the more effectively you will complete your tasks. You have a fantastic profession that requires you to use your intellect while also having a good time. When you see yourself becoming tight, take some time to relax. Make sure you take a few seconds to clear your head before heading back to work. Every event planner has to take a break now and again. Even though event planning is a difficult task, everyone, including your venue coordinator, depends on you to pull it off successfully. The finest event of your life may be planned and executed with careful preparation, communication, a little assistance, and a whole lot of fun.

6.3 Event Planning Ideas for A Very Tight Budget

It may be a lot of fun to throw a party. Although it is tempting to get carried away with event preparation, it is simple to find yourself spending considerably more money than you can afford before you know it. Trying to strike a balance between arranging a good event and maintaining spending within a fair budget takes much expertise and experience. Suppose you are worried about your financial situation and cannot afford the services of a professional event planner. In that case, there are various cost-effective planning choices and ideas available to make your event equally as memorable and enjoyable.

Here are a few suggestions: One simple approach to save money is to have your event during a time of day that is less expensive. When it comes to events such as weddings, birthday parties, and baby showers, scheduling them in the afternoon will undoubtedly save you money on the cost of the event. You would almost certainly have lower expenses for afternoon events that require less food and catering, such as light snacks and beverages such as punch, tea, or coffee, as opposed to evening events that require full course meals and a full bar, as opposed to afternoon events that require a full bar. Another consideration for event planning is whether or not you will need the services of a caterer. When it comes to small occasions, you could get away with doing most of the organizing and preparation on your own.

Caterers, on the other hand, may be of great aid for larger gatherings. If your event planning budget is really limited, hosting a potluck is usually the most effective way to save costs in the food department. Each visitor contributes either food or beverages, with some guests bringing salad or entrée and others bringing soda or wine. For a successful celebration, the event planner must interact with and coordinate closely with the visitors to ensure a great range of food and beverages with something for everyone. People do not bring identical dishes. This is a fantastic way to include all of the visitors in the event planning process, and guests are typically thrilled to participate and be a part of the celebration. Not only can you save money on food, but you can also save money on transportation. You may also concentrate on other aspects of the party, such as the entertainment or the décor.

You may invite parents, friends, and relatives to provide simple songs and magic acts to amuse the children during their birthday celebrations, or you can have them construct balloon animals or engage in water battles to keep the youngsters entertained. Decorations, on the other hand, do not have to be expensive. For example, you may purchase a large quantity of balloons and streamers for a children's party. Alternatively, for a garden party, instead of purchasing expensive outdoor lighting that you will almost certainly never use again, you can purchase a couple of outdoor torches and combine them with the outdoor lights that you usually use to adorn your trees and bushes on special occasions in your garden to create beautiful, soft lighting. Your visitors will not be able to tell the difference between costly and inexpensive lighting. They are unlikely to notice as long as the atmosphere is comfortable and the party is enjoyable. Putting careful consideration into the preparation of the event would help your dollar go farther while still allowing you to host an event that was very enjoyable for everyone.

Chapter 7: Monitoring the Budget

Laying down your planned budget on a cost sheet in Excel, as previously indicated, will help you to easily understand what products may be included while still staying within your budget when you begin to organize your event. It will also show you how you are spending your money, allowing you to examine other options and determine whether or not they would work within your budgetary constraints. Once your cost sheet has been completed and you have assessed your progress toward meeting your budget goals, you may decide that simple candles (real or battery operated, depending on the hotel and fire marshal regulations) provided by the hotel at no cost will suffice as centerpieces, and that the money saved can be used to fund the cocktail reception and other special touches for your guests. Your objective is to design a memorable event that includes all necessary event features while keeping within your budget. You want to be certain that you have taken all reasonable efforts to do this. Don't wait until the conclusion of your event to discover that you have significantly outstripped your initial budget estimates.

You must balance your budget as you go with your event—each time you incur new expenses or make modifications and changes, your budget should be updated to ensure no unpleasant surprises. Because each event will have its own set of event features, there is no fixed method or structure for creating a cost sheet. Start by walking through your event from beginning to finish and creating an outline for it as you begin to compile your cost sheet and estimate. Remember to include in the time for move-in, setup, rehearsal, tear-down, and move-out. Then go back and put in the numbers for the expenses. Always remember to have all of your estimates in writing before proceeding. Never accept conversational quotes as a substitute for written quotes. Today, personnel turnover is the norm rather than the exception; individuals are hired one day and fired the next. You must get formal confirmation of what is and is not covered. Make certain that your vendors are clear on this. Ask them to be explicit when it comes to elements that appear inconsequential, such as tipping—are gratuities calculated as a percentage of the whole cost, or is tipping subject to tax? That amount may build up, particularly if it impacts both food and beverage production and consumption.

In the same way, taxes on food and wine might differ—don't make assumptions. Check to see if any other expenses may be added to the final bill and be sure to account for them in your budget. Some venues may charge you for the exact amount of power that you use. Ask for the data from a recent comparable event that can offer you an estimate for your budget in such circumstances so that you may use them for costing reasons.

To make educated selections about what to include, you must keep track of your spending and keep track of your budget. As invoices arrive, be certain that nothing is paid out until they have been thoroughly scrutinized. Ensure that what is presented corresponds to what has been agreed upon, and that there are no surprises. Make the necessary adjustments to your cost sheet. Upon receipt of each bill, note the actual amount on your cost sheet and compare it with the estimates you made in advance to see whether they are correct. Is there anything on your final bill that you did not include in your first estimate that you want to mention? Always keep a close eye out for products that have been charged but not yet negotiated and signed off on. If an item has been overestimated, you must determine how it will affect your bottom line as soon as possible so that you may make budget modifications in other areas to make up for it before your event takes place. One event planner miscalculated the expense of mailing the invitation packages to attendees since the final package was larger than the standard size as initially planned, resulting in an unanticipated $15,000 charge for shipping the invitation packets. As you get from the creative planning phases of your event to the actual operation, you may find that the objects you had initially intended to include in your event are no longer appropriate. When planning your event, you can decide to serve your guests a specialty cocktail that requires the rental of specialised glassware, rather than the normal open bar with readily accessible glassware that you had originally planned to serve them. This would influence your budgetary estimates.

The pennies build up to dollars one by one, and the dollars may swiftly add up to thousands of dollars. If you do not maintain your cost sheet up to date, you may realize that you have exceeded your budgetary constraints. By keeping your expense sheets up to date regularly, your budget will be close to being reconciled as you approach your event. In addition, understanding your financial situation will help you make prudent decisions, such as whether you can afford to host the bar after dinner or whether you'll have to set it up as a cash bar, which will save you time and money in the long run. Perhaps you now have enough dollars left over in your budget to add a parting present for your visitors as part of your budget.

7.1 Schedule Your Payments

Before signing a contract, you should create a payment plan to see whether or not the due dates need to be altered. If payments must be modified to accommodate your client's check runs or cash flows, hotels and other venues will cooperate with you to make the necessary adjustments. The establishment of payment schedules from both the customer and the suppliers is of critical significance. It is the responsibility of event planners to inform their clients of payment terms and conditions at the time of contracting and outline dates and amounts in the contract with time buffers built in.

Before signing contracts with suppliers—or having your clients sign contracts with suppliers in the case of clients who want their event financed so that the event planning company does not take on financial risk—you must be aware of any concerns about the payment schedule so that terms and conditions can be adjusted, if necessary, and signed off on. Your cost sheet serves as the foundation around which you will build your payment plan. Should the products you want to include or the number of planned guests change, you will need to adjust your payment schedule. Before submitting the next payment, make the necessary adjustments to the amounts. When arranging your payment plan, keep in mind to account for supplier cancellation penalties. Make certain that you have received sufficient cash to cover the cancellation fees, as well as your management fee, in the case that the event must be cancelled at any moment.

7.2 Basics of Creating Budget

A budget for an event might be quite difficult to create. When faced with a long list of bills, it might be tempting to bypass the planning stage and begin negotiating contracts with your suppliers immediately. Even though it appears to be the simplest option, failing to establish a clear budget puts you at risk of blowing your budget. Establishing a budget for your event is a critical stage in the planning process, and it should be done immediately after outlining your goals and objectives. A budget is a thorough projection of how much money will be spent on your event and when it will be spent. It assists you in maintaining control over your spending and income and determine the success of your meeting or event performance. It is impossible to overstate the significance of having a budget for an event.

When putting up your event budget, it's important to think about what financial success looks like for your event and how you want to assess it. To do this, you must compile a comprehensive inventory of all of the potential expenditures and revenues that are anticipated to arise from your event. Keep your financial flow in mind at all times. Once you've created your budget, you'll need to keep track of it and review it regularly to ensure that you stay within the limits of the resources you've allocated. Every event planner's first step is to create an event budget and make as accurate a prediction as possible about whether the event will generate a profit, a loss, or a break-even point. However, understanding what financial success means for your event may vary depending on the event and the goals you have set for it. When it comes to conferences and events, a leadership summit is frequently a loss leader.

In contrast, association events are typically profitable, and trade shows are frequently the best opportunity to profit. Before you can begin preparing your budget, you must first determine the requirements of your firm. It is more accurate to say that your event budget is a prediction or estimate of all expenditures and revenues incurred during your event.

You should plan ahead of time because you won't be able to predict all expenditures and revenues at the outset, and some of them may even vary over time. Nonetheless, it is vital to prepare your budget by considering the most regular costs and income. When creating an event budget, it is critical to distinguish between things that reflect spending and those that indicate sources of income that may be used to offset expenses. To properly predict a budget for your upcoming event, you must also differentiate between fixed and variable expenditures. One of the most difficult problems for event planners is ensuring that costs and revenues are properly managed to fulfill the financial objectives set by your organisation and correctly measure the performance of your event.

7.3 Regulate your event and an overall budget

Begin with the fundamentals: you should clearly define the sort of event you're arranging and the total budget for the event from the beginning. It is usually preferable to begin creating an event from the standpoint of your available resources rather than the other way around. Hosting a cocktail reception and have $10,000 to spend on the event? A user conference with a $200,000 budget? That's a stretch. Is it possible to have a team meeting with a $2,000 budget? Whatever the occasion, the first step is to determine how much money you have available to spend on it. A management, a finance department may provide this overall budget, or it may be derived from your budget that you oversee. While budgeting methods differ from one organisation to the next, the necessity of this stage remains constant.

7.4 Estimate Your Costs

Once you have a high-level plan and a budget in place, you can start mapping out the details of each line item. Start with the items you know you'll need – a venue, food and beverage, and marketing, for example – and work your way down the list. Once you've obtained your high-level items, it's time to get down to business with the low-level items.

No matter how much you may wish to group spending by category, the more specific your budget is, the more ordered and accurate your financial picture. As you continue to compile your complete list of line-items, you should continue to get quotations from suppliers. The advantage of taking this approach is that you can work through your list of vendors over a longer period rather than completing all of your vendor outreach at the same time – right before your final budget is due. Vendor proposals and quotes should include a breakdown of your projected line-item costs as well. This is the stage at which you should be identifying the most qualified vendors for each area of your budget and putting in place formal agreements and contracts for your event. As you make important decisions –selecting vendors, selecting a location, and selecting service providers – you are piecing together a final budget for your project.

At this point, you've signed a large number of contracts and are beginning to pay your suppliers and contractors. The next step is to put your budget into action and make sure you're still in the black financially. You should include one more line item in your budget after you've finalized it: a contingency fund. Depending on the size and complexity of the event, you may want to set aside as much as 20 percent of the total event budget for this purpose. Despite your best efforts, there is always the possibility that your budget will need to be adjusted. An emergency fund ensures that you are well prepared to deal with any changes or additional expenses that may arise and cause you to exceed your projected spending goals and objectives. This will prevent you from going over your budget consistently. It is critical to have the approval of your stakeholders for your contingency fund as well. Even though it is an emergency fund, you want the team to be aware of and prepared if you need to use it in an emergency. Prepare for the unexpected with a contingency fund to alleviate some of the stress that comes with dealing with many interconnected parts.

7.5 Review and Track Your Event Budget

The planning step, which occurs throughout the event budgeting process, is just the beginning. As previously said, not all expenditures can be predicted, and your budget will almost certainly vary during the event preparation process. As a result, it is critical to regularly assess and manage your budget. If feasible, it's a good idea to schedule a meeting with your company's accounting or finance officer to go through the budget format with them. According on the size of your firm, you may choose to speak with the owner instead. This manner, you may make certain that you are in excellent physical condition before proceeding with the event planning process if necessary. Because the needs for your meeting or event may vary, it's a good idea to confirm in advance who will have the power to spend money over the budget that has been agreed.

When it comes to coping with unexpected costs, the contingency fund that was stated previously will be quite useful. It is critical to keep track of your budget throughout the event, including the planning phases. Fortunately, there are a lot of useful technological solutions available on the market that may assist you in these endeavours, such as Expensify. One of the many ways that technology can assist you is via the real-time speed and precision that it provides for communication and collaboration with your team when it comes to achieving your financial objectives. When you move your financial systems to the cloud, you will be able to manage your financial operations from any location, at any time, without the need for any additional hardware.

Once your conference or event has concluded, you must complete the accounting process by totaling all expenditures and income. By assessing your financial performance, you will be able to demonstrate your stakeholders and learn from your mistakes and better your future event by analyzing your financial performance.

To decide whether or not your event was a success, go back to the success measurements and benchmarks you established before the event. Because of the development of new technology during the last decade, planners have been able to assess the overall success of an event in various ways. With the use of qualitative and quantitative event data, you can more accurately assess the performance of your event and demonstrate its effect. Understanding and analyzing your total financial performance is difficult, but it also presents an excellent chance to drive continual progress by carefully scrutinizing your previous efforts. Determine which measurement areas are the most significant, and then give each of these critical areas a key performance indicator (KPI) based on your priorities. Your key performance indicators (KPIs) should be selected based on their relevance to the measurement area as well as their capacity to be tracked and measured properly. After that, you may compare your financial success year after year and establish a goal for an overall aggregate evaluation of your financial performance to track progress.

Chapter 8: Venue Selection Fundamentals

Finding the ideal event venue becomes much easier once you have laid out the framework of your event vision and know all of your function space requirements—including supplier move in, setup, rehearsal, day of, teardown, and move out space requirements, as well as what to look for—and have laid out the framework of your event vision. When the location is just the correct match, you will have a strong emotional connection. When you have discovered what you were seeking for, you will have an inside, intuitive understanding that will become stronger with experience that you have found it.

The moment you step inside the indoor or outdoor venue you're considering for your event; you'll be able to eliminate locations that would interfere with your vision. Such locations will not feel appropriate. By developing a clear event vision, going to lay out your event grid (which will serve as a blueprint for you all to build your event from), and becoming intimately familiar with your space, event, and supplier requirements before you begin looking for a venue, you can ensure that whatever venue you choose will meet the list of event must-haves that you have firmly imprinted in your mind before you begin looking. Even if the architecture of the building is beautiful, or if a balcony is inviting, or if a group photo taken by a column looks fantastic, if the other aspects that you have specified as essential for the event are not there, it will be pointless to you to have the event.

8.1 Site Location

Location, location, location, as they say in real estate, is everything. The location of your event is of paramount significance; it may make or break your event depending on how well it is planned. Let us consider the case of a senior exhibition held in a large convention centre divided into two sections: the north wing and the south wing. Although the north wing is older, it provides convenient access to the ballroom. There is plenty of parking available nearby. However, even though the south wing is newer, it is more than a 20-minute walk from the parking lot. This particular exhibition was held in the south wing of the building, but given the intended audience of seniors, the north wing would have been a more appropriate location. In addition, a large garden show was held in the south wing, where guests could purchase plants of all sizes and varieties. For the second time, it was not the most convenient option for the guests and exhibitors, who had to walk from the parking lot to the ballroom and back again, often with heavy purchases or boxes in tow. This was especially difficult because a convention centre does not provide bellman assistance with boxes, as a hotel does. The lesson can be physically exhausting for both attendees and exhibitors, and it can also be financially draining for the latter.

In this case, it resulted in low attendance and, in this case, low sales of plants because the plants were too heavy for most guests to carry back to their cars on their own without assistance. Make sure that the location of the event corresponds to the type of event. Look for ways to make it as convenient as possible for your visitors. There is one large specialty show that comes to Toronto twice a year, and it is called the Toronto International Film Festival. It attracts a large number of people. Underground parking is available at the show's location, allowing attendees to leave their coats in the vehicle and walk up the escalator to be directly at the venue. The exhibition organizers provide carts to make shopping more convenient. The aisles are spacious, and there is plenty of space to move around between them. If your cart or hands grow too full from carrying all of your purchases, you may drop them off at the parcel-pickup area near the main entrance. If you need assistance in transporting your items to your vehicle, please let us know.

There is lots of seating available in various locations. There are also a variety of refreshment locations, from coffee shops to water stations, to accommodate visitors of varying financial means. In addition, the venue has good restroom facilities and a diaper-changing room that is fully stocked with supplies, and the facility is wheelchair accessible. It offers everything a person might want for a pleasant experience, and people look forward to coming to the show because they know they will have a stress-free time with all of their requirements met. When choosing a location, you are not restricted to only hotels, conference centers, or eateries. Several fashionable stores will enable you to rent out their space for a private cocktail reception and supper, followed by a fashion show showcasing their latest collection of garments. Some stores even have cooking facilities adjacent to them, making it simple for caterers to set up and serve their clients' food. You may rent out yachts, roller-skating rinks, airport hangars, and even have a gala in an armory, museum, or art gallery if you want to be creative. You may have a catered event in a parking lot, on a covered tennis court, or even on the roof of a hotel if you have enough space.

Private clubs, restaurants, and even vacant warehouse space may be taken over and converted totally. Your creativity and your financial resources only limit you. You may be required to pay a premium or price to have the venue closed to the general public, and you must keep this in mind while evaluating your venue possibilities. Consider if it is financially prohibitive to rent a private space that will accommodate your visitors rather than renting out a whole building solely to satisfy your needs. The most essential thing is to discover the appropriate match for you. The mezzanine above the dining area of one restaurant that may be taken over entirely has beautiful 30-foot ceilings and four large fireplaces, making it the ideal location for a romantic winter or festive Christmas-themed wedding. Skilled event planners may acquire a sixth instinct when it comes to understanding when they have located the appropriate site for their event, one that emits the event spirit they are seeking for and fits all of the demands and logistical requirements of their event parts. The moment they enter the place, they can see it, feel it, and imagine themselves there. When they find the correct fit, they get an inner sensation of satisfaction—it feels, as Goldilocks famously remarked, "just right." Not content with second best, she sought out what was suitable for her needs and circumstances. And it is exactly what you should be looking for when planning your special occasions.

The changing of the seasons brings a new set of concerns and objects that should be taken into account when deciding where to go and how much money to spend. We know that we cannot forecast the weather, but we can be prepared for whatever may come our way. What matters most is the comfort of your visitors and their initial impressions of your establishment. When it comes to meetings in foreign nations, the off-season may provide some of the finest deals. Before making your reservation, think about the influence that poor weather will have on your itinerary if it is not optimal. Traveling to the Caribbean or Florida during hurricane season or Arizona during the summer months when flash floods and electrical storms are not recommended. Before making a final choice, check with local tourist information centers to learn about the weather in the area in the past, including temperature, precipitation, and humidity. Inquire about receiving the official weather history figures, which are readily accessible. Do not merely accept a verbal account as being accurate. Even if it has never rained or snowed during the period when you will have your event, plan ahead of time for weather backup for outdoor events (it has snowed in June in Banff), and be prepared for the worst-case scenario.

Climate patterns have altered due to global warming, and they can no longer be forecast with the same accuracy as they once were. Extreme weather conditions are becoming more common, and we have seen firsthand how ill-prepared some towns have been when calamity strikes them. Make sure you are aware of the safety and security processes in place at your site and any event cancellation policies. Contract termination terms should be scrutinized with a fine-tooth comb. Make certain that your customers are informed of any fees incurred if an event is cancelled at the last minute due to an unexpected scenario, such as inclement weather or the risk of an outbreak of an infectious illness in the region, such as SARS. Today, it is critical for event planners to be aware of cancellation fees and be able to predict the financial dangers that unforeseen events may pose to their clients' businesses. They must prepare a complete risk assessment strategy with an adequate plan of action. They must be able to provide event cancellation insurance to their customers as an additional service. When arranging an outdoor event, it is always a good idea to have a backup plan in case of bad weather. If the weather looks iffy on the day of the event (or earlier, depending on event setup requirements), you will have to decide on where to begin setting up on the day of the event. Establish a deadline by which you or your customer will be required to make a definitive choice on the location of your event. Temperatures in the 90s and 100s are not a concern in certain places. Temperatures in Las Vegas may rise to over 100 degrees Fahrenheit without interfering with the show's schedule.

All of the guests are transported to their air-conditioned accommodations in air-conditioned motor buses or limos. The temperature decreases and they may have a very nice stroll down the Strip. During the day, they are comfortable in their meetings or relaxing by the pool. In any case, the hotels and casinos are all located near one another and have been intended to encourage you to remain inside. Any excursions are typically as simple as travelling from an air-conditioned hotel to an air-conditioned bus to an air-conditioned venue and then returning to the hotel. The heat does not have a significant role. The weather also impacts water temperatures and the kind of organisms that may be found swimming in them. If you plan a trip to the southern hemisphere during the summer months, be aware that you may encounter more jellyfish than you would during the winter months, when the waters are a bit colder. When organizing a meeting on a cruise ship, find out how the weather will affect your sailing—is there a period when the seas will be calmer? If so, organize your meeting around that time. For day and nighttime trips on private yacht charters, inquire about the amount of shade and shelter the boat can offer its passengers and crew. In the event of a sudden rainfall, can everyone be properly accommodated inside? Also, does the building provide appropriate sun and rain protection? Keep in mind that the weather may influence your event practically anyplace it takes place.

Make sure you're prepared. It is essential to prepare for weather backup while organizing open-air events, especially in chilly areas. An additional concern for outdoor events is the use of heaters. In southern California, many nighttime gala events are conducted on cliffs overlooking the ocean, and freestanding heaters ensure that attendees are kept exceedingly warm. If you can picture listening to the melodies of a classical guitarist while seeing silver moonbeams dance on the soft waves below, that's what you're getting here. That type of wonderful environment cannot be replicated in a ballroom. Still, even if it were possible, the location would not be ideal for a gala fund-raiser that featured a silent auction with objects on display, or if you wanted to include multimedia, staging, or speeches into your event. What is critical is that the venue is a good fit for your event and your visitors' expectations.

8.2 Venue Cost Management
It is possible to pick a physical structure or setting and a destination, and pricing considerations may be applied to both. You should consider the following factors while planning an event outside of your own country: If so, will you need to pay for overnight airport accommodations as well? Whether or whether your location has direct, nonstop flights is something to consider. If your visitors are needed to

change planes, would they be obliged to wait for a significant period at their destination city? Whether or whether the entire amount of time spent travelling justifies the duration of the stay North American corporations contemplating hosting a conference in Hawaii or the Orient, for example, should consider a seven-night stay rather than a three-night visit, unless all attendees would be leaving from the west coast, since they will be dealing with two full days of travel and jet lag. From the airport to the hotel, how long does the journey take you? What requirements do you have in terms of a hotel and a location? What adjustments will you need to make to your programs to account for the time difference and jet lag? When your visitors arrive, they may have a small repast in their rooms as well as some time to settle in and get used to the new time zone, with the welcoming festivities taking place the next night when they aren't too exhausted to appreciate them.

8.3 Location Requirements

This will allow you to create a mental image of the first sequence of events and an overall vision of what should be included in the story. It will then be possible to send your grid to the various venues you consider to see whether they can satisfy all of your requirements. Consider include the needs for moving in, setting up for rehearsals and moving out. Also consider the scheduling and logistics of these activities. Visually stroll around the event venue to assess the amount of space needed for each activity. Begin by looking into availability and putting up a cost sheet of your project. Specificity is key. Having a 20-foot ceiling to handle audiovisual equipment and staging should be included on your floor plan and grid.

Additionally, provide room for pre-show setup and practice. You should also specify if you want the ballroom to be placed on a 24-hour hold so that your setup may be completed until the day of your event. If you will want dressing rooms for artists, offices for your employees, or a place to prepare or put-up exhibits, be sure to notify the venue as soon as possible so that they can reserve adequate space for you.

Following contract signing, it is far simpler to release space and scale down than attempt to operate in insufficient space. A thorough examination of all components of your event is required to ensure that as many expenditures as feasible are included in the budget preparation process. Working through this part, you will learn about the many expenses that must be included in your budget, such as street permits and off-duty police officers, as well as where and why these expenses should be included. Continue to update the costing as you go along, adding and deleting items as necessary to account for any changes in the project scope. Because, as previously stated, it is critical to be aware of where you stand at all times in terms of your proposed spending to make adjustments as needed and ensure that you have the funds necessary for the essential event elements that will help you to meet your company and event objectives—and the right location can play a role in achieving those objectives. For example, one of your event site goals may be to create the backdrop for something lavish and memorable that will be remembered for years to come, such as a symphony beneath the stars in the desert with a well-known musician who will only be performing for you and your attendees. Consider having your guests arrive via hot air balloon at sunset, with champagne waiting for them when they touch down on the ground. While planning your events, you should consider the practical aspects of your location, such as backup transportation if weather conditions or wind conditions are not favorable for the hot air balloons to take off; you should also consider the costs of your venue's infrastructure, such as parking and other infrastructure costs. Transportation costs to and from the event for guests who may prefer to travel by balloon chase car rather than riding in the hot air balloon; return transportation—hot air balloons do not travel after dark; a clear plastic tent (for visibility) as a weather backup; a cooking tent; porta-potties; the cost of having everything transported to the desert; medical assistance on call; security; lighting; heaters; electricity and backup generators; and someone to deal with any curious critters. After adding these costs to your budget, you may decide that holding the event in the middle of the desert is too expensive and that you need to consider a different idea.

You may also look at your cost sheet to see if there are any other sources of funding that could be used to support your original idea. Knowing exactly where you stand financially at any given time allows you to make informed decisions and run an event with no "surprises" during the final reconciliation stage, which could have been addressed and managed during the planning and operations stages rather than after the event has concluded. Prepare for all of your expenses ahead of time so that you can make informed choices about your future.

8.4 Hotels and Conference Centers

The price disparities between hotels and conference centers will have an impact on your spending plan. Both facilities may be excellent, but make sure you understand how they vary and what must be included in your cost breakdown before signing on the dotted line. If you want bedrooms and function space, hosting your event in a hotel may be the most cost-effective option. Because the hotel will be collecting money from the guestrooms and the food and beverage sales, concessions may be given for items such as room rental fees for setup and practice time. Hotel room rental fees are often waived for events that generate food and beverage income, so long as they are held on the actual event day and time planned to take place. Of course, this will be determined by the total amount of money spent at the hotel. Suppose you have your event in a hotel. In that case, your attendees will be able to walk to the meeting rooms, which will save them money on transportation expenses compared to staying at a hotel and attending a conference at a convention centre that is not within walking distance of the hotel. In other cases, local hotels have partnerships with conference centers that provide discounted room rates; in these cases, you will likely be negotiating with both the hotel and the convention centre individually.

You could wish to run a cost comparison to determine how much they vary from one another in terms of pricing. There are a variety of extra costs to consider in addition to the hotel rental fees. When your setup crews arrive, most hotels will enable them to park and unload their trucks, and they will make certain that they have workers on site to help with transferring the materials. (Don't forget to account for gratuities as part of your overall budget.) Hotels often provide tables and chairs for registration and display at no extra cost. They can frequently offer most specialty glasses, such as martini glasses for a special martini bar as part of your event, at no additional cost depending on the number of attendees. There is normally no extra price for room cleanliness since hotel ballrooms are usually carpeted, thus there is no additional need to bring in carpeting. Most hotels will be happy to offer you a secure storage location, and many will even replace misplaced keys at no extra fee. Day rooms or changing rooms may be arranged for setup employees and VIPs for events that are only taking place for a single day or over many days but for which no guestrooms are needed. Suppose your event will take place over several days and you want guestrooms. In that case, you may be able to negotiate and save money on things such as suites, upgraded rooms, early check-in and late checkout, one in every x number of rooms to be free, and special rates for employees. If there will be extra costs in any of these areas on top of the room rates and taxes, these must be included in your cost sheet, as well as any other hotel fees that will be charged to participants at the time of check-out. If you have any questions, please contact us.

You must figure in these additional fees into your budget or negotiate them with the hotel when the contract signing to have a clear picture of your overall room expenses. Hotels offer a wide range of services, including stocking minibars with personal requests, dry cleaning, laundry, faxing, typing, photocopying, providing extension cords through their in-house audiovisual suppliers, cell phone rentals, walkie-talkies, telephone hook-up at your registration desk, the installation of banners (which can be surprisingly expensive), and allowing you to use their computers for those last-minute changes to speeches that always seem to occur the night before the event begins. However, keep in mind that there may be a fee associated with any of the services listed above. Find out in advance whether there will be any additional costs for add-ons, and make sure that any expenditures submitted to the master account are approved. Make sure you note on your copy what the charge was for so that you may put it on your reconciliations and receive approval from the individual who was allowed to add on this item to your account. When organizing an event, is it worth your time to travel to the local copy shop to make copies or send a fax? That's a combination of money and common sense. Hotels will present you with a list of the services they provide, as well as an estimate of the fees associated with those services. Include these expenses as much as you can in your budget whenever possible.

For example, if you know you will want telephones at your hospitality desk, you must factor in the expenses of connections as well as the pricing for local calls (which may vary from hotel to hotel; some hotels will charge nothing while others may charge more than $1.00 per call). This is something you should estimate and include in your prices, since the money may mount up rapidly and cause your budget to be thrown out the window. There may also be obligatory taxes and service charges that must be computed and placed on top of the actual add-on price in addition to this and other types of additional expenses. Add-on charges for function space rental and private food and beverage functions may not be explicitly stated in your contract. Still, they may be referred to as "all applicable charges" in various hotel materials, such as group catering menus, which may include terms and conditions in the back, such as fees for chefs, servers, and bartenders.

If your guaranteed guest count decreases and you wish to continue using the same room (please note that the hotel reserves the right to relocate your group), add-on power drop charges for any additional electricity consumed by your audiovisual company, or union fees in the case of function space rental are all possible. Before you sign the hotel contract, you should understand precisely what costs may be incurred, get them documented, and consider how they will affect your overall budget before you sign the agreement. None of this is necessarily true when it comes to convention centers. Off-loading of products may result in labor charges. In certain cases, you may be looking at three- or four-hour minimums, overtime prices, and union fees in addition to other costs associated with the process. Tables, drape, and skirting may be subject to additional fees. Some convention venues may not have specialty glasses available, and it may be necessary to bring them in at your expense.

One corporation that advertised a martini bar at their event was conducting their event at a convention centre, rather than a hotel, for the first time in the organization's history. It turned out that they had to pay more than $6,000 in martini glass rental costs! In certain cases, carpeting is not provided for exhibit space, and renting carpet is extra. There may be additional fees associated with cutting keys and cleaning a display during a trade show. Examine the contract in detail—and in writing—to determine what is and is not covered, where there is opportunity for negotiation, and what additional expenditures will be incurred in addition to the basic charges. Having completed your cost comparisons, you will be able to determine whether a hotel or a convention centre is the most cost-effective location for your event, and you will be able to address particular concerns with the venue if necessary.

Some leasing fees may be waived by the convention centre and/or the hotel, but for them to do so, they must know how much money you will be spending at their facility in terms of guestrooms, food and beverage consumption. If your attendance numbers decline at either a hotel or a conference centre, be prepared for rental prices to climb. This will be spelled out in their agreement with you. Pay close attention to this area since it has the potential to have a significant influence on your budget.

8.5 Restaurants, Private Function Spaces, and Catering

You may opt to have your event somewhere else than a standard ballroom location to make it more memorable. Museum, art gallery, theatre of the performing arts, private estate home, heritage building, unique restaurant, airport hangar, yacht club, racetrack, local attraction and entertainment area, elite nightclub, skating rink, enclosed tennis court, indoor volleyball facility, golf club, retail store, aquarium, converted warehouse, armory, film studio, boat charter, luxury car dealership, garden, the desert, or the beach might be a better fit. According to one report, even the ocean has been employed as a venue for a white-glove-service cocktail reception and dinner, with guests sitting at tables in their bathing suits (while the waitstaff wore formal clothes) amid the South Pacific. The only limitations to the number of possible locations are your creativity and financial resources. Inquire with your facility about other locations where they have exclusive rights to serve off-property events. Some hotels have wonderful private homes with gorgeous gardens that they may rent out for special occasions to parties staying at their establishment.

The hotel continued to collect revenue dollars from rental, food, and beverage sales, and the visitors were given the option to enjoy a unique location outside of the hotel. When contemplating conducting your event in a non-traditional event site, you must research and include all relevant and logistical expenditures in your cost sheet summary from the beginning, just as you would with any hotel or convention centre rental facility. Remember to imagine every part of your event, from beginning to finish, to precisely estimate the costs of every single event piece that will be necessary, such as porta-potties in a desert location. There are several ways in which theaters—both movie theatres and stage theaters—can be used for special events of all kinds. You may hire space in some of the newer theatres to host your event, and some will even enable you to have your cocktail reception or sit-down meal directly onstage, as previously noted. You could elect to host your whole event beneath the theatre's roof, or you might decide to hold the opening event at the theatre followed by a reception at a different location.

Alternatively, you may begin with dinner at a different place, give transportation to the theatre, and then return to the original spot for cigars, coffee, liqueurs, and desserts before the show. If you think about putting your event at a theatre, make sure you go around the whole facility with your team. Find out how many seats are blocked, damaged, or otherwise useless to determine the real capacity. Take a look behind the scenes. Check to see that all fire exits have been cleaned entirely. You may be astonished to learn that these aren't the case. Although you would be even more astonished if the fire marshal decided to shut down your event because you failed to double-check the permits. When one of the event planners unlocked the fire escape doors, he saw rubbish heaped to the ceiling and blocking both exits. It was discovered that employees were throwing rubbish down a laneway rather than disposing of it properly during the winter months. Not only was the alley a fire threat, but it was also necessary for the move-in process. The rubbish was removed at the request of the event organizer, and the theatre power washed the path to the street to remove the stench and stains that had accumulated there.

Determine if the theatre is unionized, whether it is a live performance venue or a movie theatre, what laws and regulations must be adhered to, and what expenditures will be incurred and where they will be incurred. Find out when the theatre will be available for you to put up your equipment. What are the expenses associated with renting a theatre, staffing it, and bringing in a cleaning crew? Ensure that everything is functioning before a preview screening by doing a run-through before the event. Investigate how much it will cost to bring in a projectionist the day before the event to play the film, and be sure to account for these expenses in your overall budget. When one film was seen, it was discovered that there was a ten-minute gap in the middle of the picture. The film was initially scheduled to include an intermission, but it was decided to show it without a break this time around. It was necessary to cut and splice the reel. Other reasons to preview a film include checking the film's quality and screening it for dirt and rips, among other things. If a film is coming from outside the nation, be sure you provide enough time to pass customs before screening it. It is preferable to have it in your possession well in advance of your event rather than risk having it held up at customs on the day of your event. Check with the individual film companies to find out about their film rights and any fees that may be charged. Some businesses have local representation, and they may help you with the logistics of importing the film into the country. The theater's management may also give you with names and phone numbers of people to contact. Aside from changing the marquee, other ways to ensure a successful film event include rolling out the red carpet (or whatever color carpet is most appropriate—these days "red" carpets come in a variety of colors and custom designs), having existing carpets cleaned, and having the floor washed (if applicable). Beverage glasses and popcorn bags with bespoke logos are available.

Consider the time of arrival. Are people arriving with tickets and invites, or are they just showing up? Consolidate two lines to reduce congestion and needless waiting. What kind of signs will you require? Is it necessary to bring in registration tables, curtains and skirting, or tables for the drinks to the event? Everyone will come at the same time. Do you have any idea how long it will take to make popcorn for 700 people, wrap it, arrange those bags in little shopping bags with additional giveaways, and then set all of that on each movie-going chair? Don't wait until the day of the event to find out the answer to this question. Discuss the setup and distribution of the beverages. Do you need the removal of candy displays or the filling of candy displays with a certain product? Is it necessary to use ropes and stanchions? Do you have a sign that says "private party"? What strategy will you use to deal with cinema regulars? When posting the name of a movie on the marquee, do you have someone to take the phone calls that will come in due to the announcement? Do you anticipate the need for crowd control? Searchlights? Any particular theme or entertainment handouts will there be this year? Provide transportation for visitors that need to be shuttled between more than one site, if applicable.

When many visitors are coming, exiting, and proceeding to a secondary destination at the same time, do you need to put in traffic control? Consider the effects of congestion and lines, as well as how to prevent them in all situations. Will the theatre be accessible to the general public for a later movie or theatre seating, or will it be exclusively yours throughout the night? The location where those who have purchased tickets for the late performance will wait should be discussed in advance if the theatre will be offering late seating. You want to ensure that the lobby area and restrooms remain free until all of your visitors have left. Before signing the contract, be certain that it states that no one else will be let inside the theatre until your event has concluded and the theatre has been emptied of guests. Finally, but not least, he ensures that all expenditures are considered while developing your budget.

8.6 Transportation

Transportation is just as important as the other elements of your event. You must use your imagination to ensure that getting to the event site is a pleasurable experience, whether you travel by air, land, water, or even a combination of all of these modes of transportation, which is possible in some destinations and venues. Always search for methods to make the experience as pleasurable as possible, rather than just seeing it as a means to an end. Events that need visitors to be moved from one site to another might provide a unique creative challenge. When attending an event in Singapore, visitors were carried from one site to another in a novel fashion; they were met by an array of rickshaws that had been waiting outside. The rickshaws given for each visitor were identified by the themed T-shirts worn by the runners. More conventional motor coaches completed the return journey. There may be occasions when you will need to be creative with your parking and transit arrangements. Is there somewhere else you can park in the area? What shopping malls or other locations with vast parking lots are nearby that you could hire out for a few hours? The use of shuttles to transport your guests to and from the venue will eliminate any parking issues. Make them more enjoyable by using double-decker buses, school buses or, in certain cases, charter ferries or boats to transport them. In Key West, visitors may be transported from one site to another using open-air "conch" trains during "progressive" evenings, including drinks at one location, dinner at another, and finally a bustling nightclub.

However, always inform your visitors of what they may anticipate in advance. Incorporate clear instructions into your invites to ensure that they are received. Air transportation (private jets, private air charter, commercial aero planes, helicopters, hot air balloons); land transportation (limousines, private cars (road rally), motor coaches, private trains; and water transportation (private boat charters, private barges) are all options for event transportation. Always exercise caution and consideration when selecting a mode of transportation and when and how many times you are physically moving your participants. Guests arriving from a long flight and being transferred to their hotel via limousine or motor coach, for example, may not be eager to step into another vehicle the same evening to be transported to the location of the arrival dinner. That would be an excessive amount of movement in a single day. Better still, have an informal welcome reception at the hotel and give visitors the choice of retiring early so that they may wake up refreshed and ready to participate in their programs with a more relaxed state of mind.

You may put those funds aside and use them to pay for the following night's meal, which will serve as their formal welcome party for them. If that is not a possibility, a more relaxing alternative to being detained in traffic merely to be carried again in a motor vehicle would be to investigate other forms of transportation for your guests to their event. In one instance, a boat was chartered to bring guests straight from their waterfront hotel to an upscale restaurant that the yacht could dock right next to. They planned the boat transfer at twilight and transformed it into a sunset cocktail celebration, a delightful start to their programs. Motor coaches were employed for the return transfers, but by that time, the guests were comfortable and ready to just return to their rooms and rest for the night, which was exactly what they did. Suppose your event is taking place in your hometown and your guests will be driving themselves there. In that case, transportation needs might also play a significant role in determining the optimal location for your event.

It is important to consider where your event will be held to make the most logical logistical sense. Suppose you are having a client appreciation event, and your customers live in the suburbs. Does your choice of site necessitate bringing them into the city centre? Is it likely that all of your visitors will arrive by car? When choosing a site, it is important to consider parking and the transportation options available to your attendees. Is there access to public transportation? What is its accessibility like, and how late does it run? You may need to adjust your event timetable to accommodate transit schedules. Suppose you want to address your guests after dinner and the final commuter train leaves at 9 p.m. How many guests will leave right after dinner to catch that train? Whatever means of transportation is chosen, it is critical to consider the transfer as an event inclusion, treat the transfer with the same care and attention to detail as you would the actual event, and include any pertinent expenditures in your budget.

In the same way that there might be hidden charges in accommodations, there can also be hidden prices in transportation. A "barn to barn" fee may apply, which is the cost of transporting your vehicle from where it is stored to your pickup point and back again. This fee might apply to a limousine, an executive motor coach, a moving van, or any other kind of vehicle (for storage). Alternatively, you might incur minimum rental fees, such as a four-hour minimum rental fee, as well as fees for petrol, insurance, detailing, personnel, and other expenses.

Chapter 9: Food Arrangements & Guest Arrival

A party's food and beverage offerings might be the primary attraction, as in a gourmet wine- and food-tasting theme party, or they can be used as creative eye candy, an intriguing culinary centerpiece, an interactive icebreaker, or even as a sweet, tempting take-home present for guests. Think of red tablecloths with centerpiece platters made of brilliant, glittering red candy apples that have been coated in M&Ms to create a joyful atmosphere that will appeal to both children and adults alike. Alternately, apples that have been dipped in thick, creamy, gooey caramel and sprinkled with milk and white chocolate may be displayed as a centerpiece on deep, rich brown linens for an autumn celebration. Your centerpiece will transform into edible artwork by the end of the evening if you use products such as delicious candy apples instead of flower arrangements at your next party. With clear cellophane bags placed at each place setting, your guests will be able to take home a delicious memento of the evening to savor at their convenience.

The use of food stations may be strategically placed around a room to lure people in and encourage them to move about the space, mixing and mingling, as opposed to having them sit in one place and have drinks and appetizers served to them by waitstaff. The right time and location for both is important considerations. Food and beverage style and service can be seen as staging tools that may orchestrate and bring about a certain guest reaction designed to accomplish a corporate and event goal. Consider the numerous types of event energy that food and beverage and how they are presented might contribute to your event. People tend to cluster at the bar when alcohol service is not given, and they prefer to stand in one place when strategic planning is not a part of the mix. The goal is to design icebreakers that will pull people into the room while setting up action food stations, beverage stations, and entertainment staging to get people talking and connecting.

9.1 Food and Beverage Considerations

You should not feel restricted to the menus available for your event, regardless of whether it is a standing reception or a formal sit-down dinner. The majority of hotels, restaurants, and caterers are eager to collaborate with you to develop a unique menu that fits within your financial constraints. At one occasion, the dessert consisted of ice cream fruits, which were ice cream in the form, color, and taste of different fruits in various combinations. Guests raved about it after they departed, and several contacted the following day to inquire about them. Even though the ice cream fruits were of modest cost, their impact was significant. The kind of inspired creativity you are seeking for is exactly what you will find here. Consider the fortune cookie cake made by a well-known caterer, which includes personalized inscriptions in the fortune cookies. Look for distinctive things. What can you do to demonstrate flare, originality, ingenuity, and personal style? Consider the sort of cuisine you will be serving before you begin. Always remember to provide vegetarian options in your menu.

Make sure to include a section on your registration forms that asks about specific meal preferences and food allergies so that you can use this information to help you prepare meals. Before the event, you will need to know how many of your guests are vegetarians, how many are allergic to shellfish or peanuts, and so on. Most of the time, special meals may be made to fit their individual needs and preferences. If you are hosting a stand-up reception with hot and cold hors d'oeuvres that will be handed around, make sure that they are bite-size and can be handled easily—no bones or dripping sauces please! Do you think people will be eating them with only a napkin or will there be plates? Will there be any delays because there aren't enough plates for numerous courses, or will there be delays because the plates are being cleaned and brought back out again? The same is true for glasses used for specialised beverages. Is there a sufficient number of glasses on hand at the site, or do glasses need to be brought in and budgeted for separately? You must make certain that you ask the appropriate questions and that you are comfortable with the answers. If you advertise a martini bar as part of your event and then discover the day before the event that the venue does not have martini glasses in stock, you will have lost some credibility in the presentation of your event.

It is possible that you may be trying to locate rentals at the last minute and will have to pay premium fees. It would also hurt your financial expectations. You will need to provide the caterers with an accurate count of how many meals they will need to prepare in advance. This is referred to as a food guarantee, and it may be a difficult business to navigate. If you promise 100 dinners and only 50 people show up, you will be responsible for the full cost of all 100 dinners as well as the cost of 50 extremely costly "doggie bags." Because of late RSVPs and no-shows, the guarantee becomes a balancing act. Instead of being plagued by no-shows, you can find yourself dealing with the inverse problem: unexpected visitors. This is when the concept of "overage" comes into play. In the case of overage, you must still guarantee a specific number of meals, but the facility will prepare additional meals in the event of last-minute cancellations. You may be able to reduce your guarantee by 5 to 10%.

Even while you will be charged according to the actual numbers, you may be able to save money if you have last-minute cancellations or no-shows. Identify the people who will be attending as guests and who will be required to sign a food guarantee. Are staff, stage and lighting personnel, entertainers, photographers, and media members included as guests, or would separate arrangements need to be made for each of these groups? If you provide them with food, be certain that these expenses are included in your estimated budget. Perhaps the most important guideline of planning a special event is to ensure that there are always enough bartenders available. Second rule of thumb: make sure you have enough booze on hand. It is humiliating to run out of food. And think about where you want your bars to be positioned carefully. You want to avoid standing in line and being stuck in traffic.

Is it necessary to charge you each drink, or is it possible to negotiate a fixed rate? Is it necessary to seek any specific permissions to operate a bar or prolong the operation hours? Should the area where beverages will be served be closed off or open to the public? Are there any guidelines you should follow regarding the kind of beverages you offer (such as shooters or pricey brandies and wines) while the host is picking up the tab? Guest may get inebriated drinking shots in a short period, especially when competitions begin, and your bar bill can soon rise to unsustainable levels. Rare brandies, ice wines, and champagne are all pricey, and if everyone wishes to try them, it may significantly influence your overall expenditure. Provide specific directions to the bartenders and waiters on how you would want them to respond to requests for such foods and beverages. You may select that visitor will be informed that they are welcome to enjoy champagne or specialised products, but that they will be responsible for the cost of these things. Alternatively, you may determine that, even if it is not being marketed or made available publicly, it is acceptable to accommodate a particular request made by a visitor. Be it more important to you that the waiters serve the wine or that the bottles are left on the table if wine is included with the dinner?

Is the number of bottles each table infinite, or is there a defined number of bottles per table? What procedures are in place to deal with requests for more wine over the allotted amount? You should include a provision in your budget for tipping the employees. A particular proportion is used to compute gratuities, which are then billed to your master account in the majority of cases. Because the proportion changes from place to event, you must inquire in each instance. In certain locations, a government tax is levied on the amount of money that is being tipped. These pennies may not seem to be a significant factor, but they may pile up over time. If this is the case, be sure to account for it in your budget calculations. Don't make the mistake of assuming that taxes on food and beverages are the same. If you plan on bringing any products into the facility, be sure to inquire about the "corkage" fees.

Providing your wine or liquor will result in an additional charge of this amount. At fund-raisers, a sponsor who is also a winemaker may provide the wine to be served, and the venue may charge a corkage fee to cover the cost of serving the wine. Ask the beverage manager to notify you when you have reached the halfway point of your expected budget so that you can determine whether or not to slow down service. Make certain that the crew does not commence takedown until you have permitted them to do so. This applies to both food and bar service operations. You may have to be adaptable. The customer can opt to prolong the party if things are going well and the attendees don't want it to stop while everything is in full gear. Find out about overtime fees— what would be charged if you opted to keep the celebration going longer? Make sure that everyone on the team knows that this is a possibility in advance of the event.

9.2 Guest Arrival

The entrance of guests sets the tone for the next event by creating an atmosphere of anticipation. Your event does not begin when the visitors enter the venue, but rather when they arrive at the venue's front door or the authorized parking drop-off spot. The weather they could experience while getting out of the car, the look and feel of the pathway to the venue, and what they will see to indicate visually that they have "arrived" at the event are all things that need to be planned and prepared for. In addition to fanfare and unique meet-and-greet touches, arrivals may vary from simple—but still demonstrating care and attention to detail and creating the mood—to spectacular and replete with special effects. Each of the event guest arrival parts has its own set of schedule and logistical needs (venue, supplier, and guest), as well as its own set of financial and creative considerations. In the case of an incentive or conference programs, they apply to arrivals at the airport, hotels and resorts, and arrivals at each event within the programs. Consider the possibility of generating energy at the arrival area.

What do you want the appearance and feel to be like? Not a drab, flat, and listless entrance, but one that builds up excitement and suspense. You want your guests to feel as if they have reached someplace exceptional and that there is a buzz of excitement in the air as they enter your venue. You may generate energy by engaging the senses of your visitors in as many different ways as possible.

One event planning business successfully employed affordable lighting to generate movement using moving bespoke gobos to guide the way into the main space, saving money in the process. "Gobos are silhouette patterns made from metal or glass that are used to project pictures from a light fixture [spotlight] onto any surface—this might be the wall, dance floor, ceiling or drapery—and they can be static [stationary] or dynamic and move about the area." Adding elements such as music, entertainment, and special effects may help create a sense of anticipation that something fantastic is about to happen. When you host unique events in different nations or areas, make a special effort to meet your visitors when they step off the airport or arrive by car. Look into what can be done at a minimal cost or even as part of the local tourist board's promotional budget by contacting the local tourist board. Often, they can arrange for a local band to greet guests while they are waiting to be processed through immigration checkpoint. A welcome banner can be displayed, and a complimentary local beverage can be served. In reality, greeting arriving guests is not the first step; rather, the first step occurs at the originating airport from which guests are departing and includes items such as those discussed previously, such as arranging for an exclusive group check-in, having someone provide luggage carts for your guests' convenience, and possibly setting up a private room with refreshments reserved for your group if airport regulations permit it. In addition, pre-boarding and group seating should be coordinated whenever and wherever possible to ensure that your guests can all sit together comfortably. This is also beneficial to the other passengers as they will not be disturbed throughout the flight by people talking across from one another in the aisle.

In addition to these activities, there are other options available on board the aircraft. Welcome-aboard announcements, custom-printed headrest covers, food and beverage vouchers, and movie and headset vouchers are just a few of the options available. Additionally, depending on the number of participants and availability, groups may sometimes be upgraded. If the whole group is unable to be upgraded, you have the option to refuse the offer in this case. Because only a limited number of first-class tickets were available, one incentive organisation conducted a random drawing to choose who would be promoted to first class. Keep in mind that attendees will be expected to dress properly for the occasion. Many VIPs do not want to sit in first class while the rest of the party is in coach, and vice versa. Visitors in high-ranking positions who prefer first-class travel often book a separate flight and arrive at the destination ahead of their visitors. Several goods may be bargained for with the airlines before signing the contract, or they can be made accessible at a low cost to customers.

These policies and procedures should be included in your function sheets and reviewed again before the group leaves. As soon as tourists arrive at their location, they must get exposed to a little bit of local culture. A lei, steel drums, and fruit punch (with or without rum), as well as local beers such as Red Stripe and Banks, are all appropriate ways to be greeted in Hawaii, Jamaica, and Barbados, among other places. On the shuttle, provide beverages and cold towels, and at the hotel, arrange for a special group check-in that is only open to group members. It is expected that envelopes containing keys to their rooms and minibars, as well as general hotel information and express checkout forms, will be available for them when they arrive. At this stage, credit card imprints for incidentals may be obtained to pay the event's costs. Because of this arrangement, they will not have to wait in line with the rest of the approaching visitors. When hosting a party in a hot region, it is beneficial to have ice-cold water, fresh lemonade, and iced tea ready for guests when they arrive. Many hotels in the Caribbean provide clients with ice-cold towels and beverages as they check into their establishment.

Clean facecloths may be dipped in lemon water, wrung off well, and placed in separate plastic bags to be frozen before being transported to the airport in coolers by the hotel employees. While many hotels throughout the globe claim that they are unable to accommodate private group check-ins, the truth is that they can and do. Persist in your efforts. Having travel-weary customers stand in long check-in lines when they might instead choose to wait in a private room with refreshments and a private check-in is just unacceptable. As long as the flight arrives before their rooms are ready (and other guests have not checked out yet), it is a simple matter to arrange for a day room where clients can change, leave their carry-on luggage in a safe and secure area, and then go out to enjoy the hotel's amenities. It is important to note that their checked baggage will be handled separately by the bell staff and delivered straight to their rooms after their rooms have been allocated. Check with your security personnel to check that a member of your team is assigned to monitor the guest day room and visitors' belongings.

This space is suitable for the installation of a hospitality desk. The event planner must make all efforts to ensure that the guestrooms are ready for use as soon as possible. This includes requesting additional maid service in advance, providing the hotel with an arrival schedule well in advance so that the rooms can be assigned according to flight arrival time and requesting early check-in whenever possible. As long as your budget permits, you may reserve the rooms for the evening before your company comes, ensuring that they are ready for rapid check-in when they arrive. It is also possible to meet with the rooms manager the night before the group arrives to determine how many rooms are available and which ones you can begin pre-assigning the following morning. Don't wait till the following day to get started.

CONCLUSION

Congratulations on finishing the book! The last of the guests has left the premises. Your event has come to an end. Keep in mind that only you and the others engaged in the planning and execution of the project will know whether or not everything went as intended. You may have had some unexpected twists and turns throughout your event, but isn't that what life is all about? If you have managed to tackle the obstacles calmly, serenely, and with a grin on your face, no one will be able to tell what was going on behind the scenes. Keep in mind the picture of a swan beautifully floating on water while its feet are paddling fiercely under the surface. Even if it is just for a few minutes, make an effort throughout the event to relish every second of it before moving on to the next thing on your function schedule.

Remember to note any observations on your function sheets so that you can refer to them later. They will serve to refresh your memory when you sit down for your final inspection. If at all possible, prepare to do nothing except pamper yourself the next day. The day following an incident always has an emotional effect on those who witness it. You have poured your heart and energy into it, worked tirelessly day and night to see it through to completion, and now it is done. Sometimes it takes a year to plan anything, and other times it takes three weeks, but you are almost certainly fatigued by the end of it. It's a good opportunity to take stock of the situation and luxuriate in the success of a well-executed event.

For further information keep in touch with us.

Visit our website : https://www.vinneumont-events.com/

VINNEUMONT EVENTS

Tel.: 0203 086 9983

10 – 16 Tiller road,

E148PX

Enquiries@vinneumont-events.com

Good Luck!

REFERENCES

- The authors (G.C. Ramsborg, B Miller, D Breiter, B.J. Reed, & A. Rushing) (eds), Professional meeting management: Comprehensive techniques for meetings, conferences, and events, Kendall/Hunt Publishing, Dubuque, Iowa, 2008, 5th edition.
- "The ten most and least stressful occupations in the United States of America." www.cbsnews.com.
- Bruno Schivinski, Daniela Langaro, and Christina Shaw are among the authors of this article (2019). "The Influence of Social Media Communication on Consumers' Attitudes and Behavioral Intentions Concerning Brandsponsored Events." This study was conducted by the University of Michigan. Management of events.
- This article is titled "What You Should Know About New Degrees in Event Management." BizBash, November 21st, 2017.
- "Program: Event Management (B.S.) - University of Central Florida - Acalog ACMSTM". ucf.catalog.acalog.com. "Program: Event Management (B.S.) - University of Central Florida - Acalog ACMSTM".
- "Events Management Degree Concentration | SRST" is the title of this page. srtm.gmu.edu.
- At catalog.ufl.edu, you may find information on Tourism, Events, and Recreation Management at the University of Florida.

- "Events Industry Council > CMP > About CMP" is an abbreviation. www.eventscouncil.org.
- "Learning Program for the CEM® (Certified in Exhibition Management®) Certification." IAEE.

Printed in Great Britain
by Amazon

17465724R00045